Hold on Kids

A Collection of Short Stories

Beverley Clarkson

BURKWOOD
Media Group

Dedication

This book is dedicated to my mother, Daphne, who provided the love, directions, vision and sense of adventure in our lives; my older brothers, Orlando and Norman, who were so essential to my life as a youngster. Orlando always looked out for me and made sure that I was taken care of. Norman provided me many ways in which to look at this new world. Eddie and my younger sisters embraced our childhood, as well as our father, the Reverend Norman Matthews, who started us on this journey to America.

Thank You

I would like to extend a special "Thank you," to my publisher Debra Funderburk for her help in the organization of my book and editing.

I am also endlessly grateful to my husband Clarence and my daughter Mia for their tireless reading, suggestions, and preparations.

I especially would like to thank my daughter for the graphic details shared, in her own words, of her experience during the 1994 earthquake in Los Angeles.

Acknowledgment

I would like to acknowledge the support of my Santa Monica Writing Group for their willingness to read some of my short stories, helping me to make sense of my memories, while clarifying questions a reader may have.

Table of Contents

Preface

Within the circumference of my mind, I see three-square objects spinning, kind of orange in color, and recognize I've had this same dream before, and wonder why it keeps reoccurring. In the foreground, I see my two older brothers holding my hand. I'm just a little girl. In the background are my parents, not standing together, but they are there. I hear my mother's voice and turn my head to look. She stands proudly with a confident smile as she gestures to us to go on while shouting, "Hold on Kids!" I hold my brothers' hands tighter, anticipating the road may be different ahead, and her words are really a warning. My brothers look down at me, faces bright, strengthened by our mother's confidence, we move on.

My mother's words echo in my ears, initially perturbing, making me feel leery of what we may encounter. But as her words encircle my consciousness, the words become soft like an endearment. She shouts, because she wants to make sure we can hear her words in the swirl of wind whisking past her. I am comforted as we venture forward in the warm grasp of my brothers' sturdy hands. I turn back, one last time to see her, but I must keep moving, because this path is different, and I am not familiar with it. I notice the bleached top stone pavers as we walk into the brilliant sunlight. They are not easy to walk on, and I am wearing red patent leather shoes, like the ones my mother said I took my first steps in as a toddler.

I barely notice my father in my peripheral vision, grounded firmly in his rigid belief system. I just thought he was plain mean; but he is there, looking tenderly at us. My oldest brother, Orlando, is excited about our excursion. My other brother Norman seems a little more apprehensive. Orlando tells us to hurry so we won't miss out. I look up at his pleasant round face, dark brown eyes bright with anticipation, and join him in his captivating excitement. He is after all my big brother and he will look out for me. This will be an adventure!

I smile as I relish the thought.

***

My two older brothers and I were born in Kingston, Jamaica British West Indies, as were my parents. We came to America in 1950 with our mother. My father had already established residency in Indianapolis, Indiana and attended Butler University as a divinity student.

In America, three more children were born making our family a total of six children and two adults. I am almost ten years older than my youngest sibling, Yvonne. This book focuses on the children who were born in Jamaica, because we probably experienced the greatest transitions. My youngest brother Eddie, born the next year after our arrival in America, is also included in some of my episodes. As for my two younger sisters, including Elaine the middle child, most of my memories are of babysitting my sisters; not really enough details for writing childhood memories. Then I was off, away in college and later married.

Our mother died in 1988 from congestive heart failure and my father passed away in 1998 after a fall in his backyard which left him weak, changing his life from one of independence to dependence on my younger sister. In the hospital, I said to him, "Well Daddy, (the American way, not 'Daw-de' as we would say in Jamaica), how did it feel to sleep under the stars?" My father was never an outdoors man. He laughed hardily. I was with both of my parents when they passed, for that I will be forever grateful. They both waited for me to return to my childhood home in Indiana, before transitioning into the next realm. I was with my mother on an airplane when she passed.

This is the third book in my trilogy about my family. The first is entitled, *"It's of No Consequence,"* the story of my grandmother. The second is *"Rightfully Hers,"* my mother's story, and this last book, *"Hold on Kids!"* is basically short stories of my early years with my brothers. I have embellished it with stories of my life as an adult.

Part One

In My Life

Hold on Kids!

The last time we were all together as siblings was a solemn occasion. The air that August day was balmy and thick. My chest rose in sync with the minister's words, 'Ashes to Ashes, Dust to Dust.' We looked into each other's eyes, tears blinding my own and my sisters, as the intensity from the sun made it difficult to see. My brothers stood staunchly. Orlando, not well, but making the best of it; Norman checking his surroundings as police officers do; and Eddie imbued with the confidence of a corporate insurance agent. Our spouses, children, grandchildren, family and friends embraced us. Even one of my father's younger sister had flown in from Jamaica and spoke at his service.

In 1998, I stood with my five siblings, my father's casket exposed, as the minister tossed fresh-dug soil on top. I never liked that sound, depicting traditional finality. We were now orphans. Our mother had died in 1988.

The week before, I was with our father at my youngest sister's home, when he took his last breath. My brothers and sisters said he was asking for me and waiting for me to come, to complete the circle of life, seeing his children. I flew from California to Indiana. Yvonne's home, not far from the Indianapolis Colt Training Center, was newly built. Inside, her airconditioned home was cool and pleasant, a major contrast from the muggy summer air outside.

After the service, at Eddie's home, the entire family came together and reminisced about our childhood. Norman jumped into the conversation, trying to lift our spirits. He laughed while kidding, and said, "Beverley is the angel of death." I think he was kidding. I know he said this because I was the child with both of our parents when they died. "If I get sick, don't call Bev!" Then his laughter consumed the room and my other siblings joined in. Me too, included, but I was uncomfortable. I felt nervous, and my laugher was only to camouflage this feeling that came over me. I had no control over when our parents would die; and certainly, he knew that.

I had a lifetime of struggles with my father, no good memories, other than he always provided a roof over our heads, paid the bills and bought the food. But as a child, he was not kind, abrasive was probably a better fit. I thought he was just plain mean; but with my brothers and sisters, (I inhale the memories of our childhood together) it was special, like having a warm blanket pulled up to my neck on a cold night.

Thankfully, at this time in our lives we could take care of ourselves, with families of our own. In the world we branched out into, we understood that each of us would be alone. I could only rely on this progeny now for emotional support: rare hugs when we saw each other, phone calls, some vacation time, and prayers.

***

In my mind's eye, I see and hear our mother shouting through the vigorous wind, "Hold on Kids!" I still feel the bellows against my face and chest and the rumbling in my ears. I understood immediately what she meant and embraced her words. They provided a layer of protection, direction and love, which our mother knew we needed.

2

Scared

Growing up with the fear of the Ku Klux Klan always in the back of my mind, I was careful of being alone. I never saw any signs of the KKK, but it was important to be vigilant, because things happened.   There were girls my age, (thirteen, fourteen) who disappeared. One, a Black girl, in the ninth grade, was last seen going to high school late one morning. She was my friend in Sunday school. We always sat together and tried not to giggle at the silly things the boys said. She was a nice and easy friend to have, because she never argued with me and had a pleasant laugh. Sunday morning were always comfortable with her. She was just sweet and kind. She had lovely smooth beige-colored skin with never a blemish. Sometimes on Sundays, as we grew older, she wore a touch of red lipstick which highlighted her lips against her pale pallet. Her mother also had that same creamy complexion.

Her family never saw her again. I thought about her every day, as I prepared to go to high school. What if the KKK had gotten to her and tortured her? I looked the landscape for her, hoping to see her gentle smiling face again, coming out of a store or just surreptitiously appearing on the street. Years later, skeletal remains were found and linked to her body. That news scarred me for a lifetime.

***

Indianapolis was historically a Jim Crow city. In 1965, all the signs were taken down, but there were those who did not agree with the dismantling of those laws. Although the signs were gone, our skin color had not changed, a constant reminder to those who believed that we were inferior, second class citizens, signs or not. It took a while for me to feel comfortable in restaurants, restrooms, and at water fountains. As a child, white people would stare at us while on our shopping excursions to downtown Indianapolis. My mother would stand and wait at the counter when our family stepped up to place our order. Granted, there were usually at least four of us, and open seats were hard to come by. Many times, my mother did not sit down. She just wanted her children to have seats. Some white people had pleasant faces, others appeared annoyed and anxious, like Black people were invading their space.

The newspapers kept me abreast of KKK activities from Ft. Wayne, Indiana, on to Martinsville and Evansville. I was frightened when I saw their pictures in the newspapers or on television, knowing they hated my brothers, my father (although he did not like Black men either), and me.

***

The "Ed Sullivan Show" connected my family to much of the entertainment world we did not know. Watching Elvis Presley singing "Love Me Tender," "Don't Be Cruel," and

"You Ain't Nothing but a Hound Dog" brought such gaiety to our lives. Later, the Beatles from England were on the show, singing "Twist and Shout," etc. I would have loved to scream with the girls, but my father would not permit such vocalizations in our home. In fact, if it was not for my mother, we would never have watched this show. My father thought all of this entertainment was foolishness. People should be contemplating more serious issues in life. Children should be reading books. Books were the only Christmas gift I ever got from my father. Nothing on our Birthdays.

I remember one time my father gave me fifty cents for my birthday, a rare occurrence. Later that day, the paper boy came with the bill for the month, so I paid him with my birthday money. I told my father what I did and asked for the money back. He never gave it back to me.

But on Sunday evenings with my parents, I just listened, watched and smiled. We laughed at some of Elvis' dance moves and were embarrassed by his seductive gyrations. My father thought those moves were an abomination, disgraceful. We watched Ed Sullivan's expressions. He was also taken back by those moves, while trying to be polite as the host. On Saturday afternoon, we watched American Band Stand. My father did not allow dancing in the house, so we only watched and danced along with the teenagers, when he was away running errands or between jobs. The minute our father's car rolled up to the house, his children returned to the quiet, studious kids our father desperately wanted and expected.

***

I was sitting in my high school geometry class in 1963 when our principal's voice came over the public address system. This was something he rarely did, so we perked up to listen. He announced the assassination of President John F. Kennedy. We were in shock. Over the weeks, I was glued to the television set along with my family. Seeing little John John, the President's toddler son, saluting his father's casket was so painful. In 1968, I was shattered by the death of Martin Luther King, Jr. who had visited our church in 1963 before the Civil Rights Act in 1964. My father did not think much of Dr. King. Therefore, his death had little baring on his life, or so he thought.

My mother, a Black woman, was first allowed to vote following the Voting Rights Act of 1965; not when white women and Negro women fought for those rights during the Women's Suffrage Movement in 1920. It took another forty-five years for Black women to be included, to be given the right, that was rightfully theirs as citizens. My parents were always on opposite sides. My mother was a Republican and my father a member of the Democratic Party. This was another stance to let my father know he could not control her.

I sat at our dining room table with my mother as she read about the candidates and issues coming up in the elections, pros and cons. I understood why she felt she had to stand on her own. She had been alone all her life.

I remember my father visiting the Peoples Republic of China

as part of a delegation from the United States. He did not have to pay for anything. That is probably the only reason he went. This trip made me nervous, thinking our family might be targeted. When he came back, he had accolades about communist China and about Chairman Mao. I could not believe my father did not like Martin Luther King Junior, a non-violent man, but thought highly of China. How could that be?

***

My junior year of college, April 4, 1968, I was almost euphoric, after waiting with Clarence, now my husband, and friends for hours in the new Irving Gymnasium on Ball State University campus to hear Bobby Kennedy speak. The gym was filled to capacity. Secret agents surrounded him. I was spellbound by his words and commitment to humanity. I felt a kinship, like I had a special connection to those twelve thousand students and professors packed in the gym that evening. The energy reached a boiling point where it could easily have been bottled for future generations. We were going to organize in support of his candidacy as the next President of the United States of America. I was in awe! He gave me such hope for our nation.

After the event closed, Clarence walked me to my new dormitory, Menk Hall, and we were both excited about the future. We had such optimism. I went to bed clutching my starched white pillow, school issued, with a satisfied smile on my face. As I breathed in the awaiting slumber, I knew everything was going to be alright. I slept soundly.

The next morning, I awakened to the sound of girls running down the halls. There was a lot of commotion and I quickly learned why. Bobby Kennedy was killed in Los Angeles in the Ambassador Hotel, after leaving our event at the university. A large number of us, in nightgowns and pajamas, ran downstairs to the lounge to watch the large technicolored television. I was in a fool's paradise sitting on the sofas with other girls crying. I was devastated!

***

Clarence and I had a beautiful wedding in June of 1969, even though I had a 'tug of war,' down the aisle with my father who wanted the attention. This was the first public wedding for our family, (Orlando had a shotgun wedding and Norman was married in a civil ceremony). My father paid for everything. So, I guess, it was all about him. The last week in August, we headed to California for our first teaching experience in inner city Los Angeles. Clarence drove his vintage 1953 mint green Buick and I drove my white Plymouth (which my father gave me as a college graduation gift) from Indiana to California. Both cars were packed with our wedding gifts. Only once in Oklahoma did large trucks separate us. I saw Clarence pull ahead of this massive line of trucks in rush hour traffic; but in an instant, he was out of sight. Nervously, I pulled off Route 66 to the side of the road and waited for him to find me.

Each night, I called my mother from a pay phone, so she knew we were okay. We did not have cell phones or mobile phones back then. Following our AAA map instructions and hotel reservations, it took us about five days to get to California from Indiana in August. In the evenings, Clarence rubbed my calves down to my ankles with Ben Gay, swollen from travel. I had never stayed in a motel room before and didn't know I was not supposed to make the bed, which I did before we left each morning. This still tickles me to this day.

The greatest shock on our trip, however, was the presence of heavy snow when we got to Flagstaff, Arizona. I never expected that. I was freezing, so we pulled over at a truck stop, while I pulled sweaters from my luggage. Then we waited, ate a late lunch, before continuing. The other cities in Arizona were blazing hot.

3

Joe

Our daughter Mia, an only child, was born in 1972. My best friend, Alice, and her sister came to the hospital to visit us. Both of these women were born here in LA. Now, my daughter was too. Then, LA was considered one of the cleanest cities in the world, and I was proud to live here.

My daughter was anxious to have a large family, so when the project in primary school was about 'Family,' Mia, wanting to be like the other children with siblings, talked about Joe. When I picked up Mia from school, her teacher told me Mia shared about her brother Joe with the class. The teacher noticed immediately my change in demeanor. I assured the teacher Mia did not have a brother. Joe was our family pet, a Mynah bird, who we taught to talk.

***

My niece Jean joined our family in 1978. The girls grew up like sisters. One Sunday at the dinner table, we were trying to get our niece to commit to some direction. Our daughter was probably seven and our niece was about fifteen years old. We were having a discussion about her future. Actually, Clarence and I were doing most of the talking. We asked her, "Well, just what do you plan to do with your life?" My niece held back, took another bite of food, while we waited. Being a typical teenager, she finally said, "I'll just live in the streets." Clarence and I looked at her with surprise, because she was a child who did not talk much. In fact, Mia answered most questions directed to her. However, we did not expect this response. When our daughter heard what she said, she shouted with grave concern, "You can't live in the street Jean, because you will get hit by a car!"

4

Professional Life

My first teaching experience in Los Angeles inner-city was a sprinkle of salt and lots of pepper. Needless to say, too much of either can be deadly or will certainly leave an acrid taste in your mouth. There were many days that were frustrating and yet my students gave me hope.

A couple of years later, I was selected as the discipline dean for the eighth-grade class, most of whom I knew from having them in my own classes. One day after school, we heard on our Motorola radios to lock the doors, because a pursuit was taking place in the hall. I thought this was a little strange, since school had been dismissed and there were just a few teachers, administrators and the custodial night crew on campus.

I rose quickly from my office desk and rushed to lock the door. I decided to take a quick look down the massive two city blocks long hallway, when I recognized one of my former students. He was running down the center, heading in my direction. He was a straight "A" student, so illustrious, so polite and charming. My breath caught in my throat when I saw him, because police with guns drawn were chasing him. This was a dangerous pursuit. My wonderful student was holding a sawed-off shotgun at chest level, thrust confidently forward, as he ran. I knew he saw me, as I pulled the door swiftly before he passed.

I couldn't believe my eyes, but it was him. I was crushed and frightened. Although I never thought even once he would hurt me. I was afraid he would be hurt. After all, this was not a television show. This was real life; and my marvelous junior high student, the one I imagined at MIT making decisions that would positively affect the world, was a gangster. I didn't get it. This dichotomy was overwhelming.

The next morning, I was told by the police captain my "wonderful" student was head of a known gang in the area. While he sat peacefully in my classroom, working hard, with perfect attendance, he directed and masterminded an army of students, truant from school, to do his bidding.

I felt so gullible! I was so hurt!

***

Clarence and I became school administrators in the 1980's just as crack cocaine exploded across the country in urban areas. Inner city schools were especially challenging, and the violence, both on campus and in the surrounding neighborhoods, was overwhelming. Training for this was very limited. Strategies were briefly discussed at weekly Faculty Meetings, and once a month a professional development activity (lasting 2 – 3 hours) was designated with police officers, social services representatives, and small group discussions. Weekly, students were fired on by street gangs while simply walking to school. School became their refuge, an oasis from the violence on the streets. They knew help would be available for them there. Each week, working with the school nurse, teachers and administrators, we rendered first aid until the paramedics arrived. Staff telephoned parents and guardians, and comforted students, all while continuing to provide an education. I know it is hard to believe, but this was the life of my students in South Central Los Angeles.

Usually, I was able to emotionally remove myself and compartmentalize the daily horrors and violence I witnessed. It was as if I wasn't there, just mechanically doing the job required to help students feel safe. I was inoculated, like the community around me. However, on one particular occasion, our school was on lockdown because bullets had been fired near the campus and there were reports of a girl seen running, pursued by suspects in a car. School administrators, coordinators, counselors, and campus aides, with walkie talkies, took off to patrol. This school had about three thousand students. In groups of twos, we scattered about the campus.

Nearing the faculty parking lot, I saw a body lying on the ground through the chain-linked fence, adjacent to a residential area of neatly manicured lawns with small, charming one-story houses. I, along with another administrator, went to that location. School police took off in a vehicle hoping to get the suspects. It was a chilly October morning. We got to the victim first, finding the young girl face down on the sidewalk. I stooped down to see if the student was breathing. She looked about fifteen or sixteen years old. I took off my coat and placed it over her body for warmth, because she was wearing only shorts and a t-shirt. We called for a nurse and paramedics, and when the nurse arrived, she checked for vital signs.

During the wait, I could feel rage mounting inside me. My insides were on fire. My chest felt tight, and the sensation of intense heat moved from my chest to my face. I could feel the burn and see the internal flames folding and greedily lapping over each other, wanting all the oxygen. Here was a child lying on the ground before me. A girl with a bullet wound in her back, a circle of blood surrounding the protrusion through her t-shirt, as she laid mortally wounded.

I had a young girl at home, much younger; yet look how different their lives were. I never told my daughter about the violent incidents at work. I did not want her to be afraid for me when I left for work. I thought about my child, safe at her school in Santa Monica. I knew that tragedies could happen anywhere; but the frequency in South Central was shattering. Only Clarence and my friends knew of my life at work, and my husband struggled with similar issues at the inner- city schools where he worked.

Before the paramedics left, they returned my beige all-weather coat with a zipped fleece lining. The next day we were told that she died, in a drug deal gone sour. I see her slim brown face, hair cut short in a curly pixie, and matching shorts and t-shirt. She was a child well cared for, with moisturizing lotion applied to her skin and hair cut fresh and styled. She was loved by somebody. The girl was not a student at our school. No adult knew her or had ever seen her. I am sure the students knew her, but silence was their modus operandi.

Every week Black boys fought Black boys, Latinos fought Latinos, and sometimes Blacks and Latinos fought each other. White male police arrested Black boys and men, Mexicans, Hispanic or Latin Americans. They thought boys and men of color were drug dealers and gang bangers. All across this nation, men of color were not respected by white men in authority and were generally feared by white women through the media.

***

How to integrate schools became a dominate topic for the school district. I, along with hundreds of minority teachers and fewer administrators transferred from inner city schools to the valley to support students, particularly minority students who volunteered to ride the school buses from Los Angeles to the valley as part of the desegregation process. I was now an Assistant Principal.

One afternoon at a school in San Fernando Valley shortly after lunch ended, I heard students running down the hall, calling my name. I looked up from my office desk, to see two boys running in, out of breath, yelling, "Ms. Clarkson!" One boy with a profusion of blood, running down his arm like a fountain into his armpit, shirt soaked, sticking to his chest yelled, "Help me!" His arm was above his head. The blood was bright red next to his olive skin. His ring finger, like a stop sign, was missing. I jumped up to apply pressure while taking him to the nurse, as I instructed his friend to go back and find his finger.

I was surprised the student had not gone into shock, from the distance the boys ran from the gym and the loss of so much blood. Blood trailed his path down the hallway. He was, however, still able to talk, as his face gradually began to lose color. The student was running on pure adrenaline.

The paramedics called initiated an air lift for the pupil. His friend found his finger and brought it back. The nurse placed his finger in a Ziploc plastic bag in a saline solution, awaiting the transport. His friend also brought back his gold ring, flattened like it had been pounded by a rubber headed hammer in a jewelry repair shop. His friend told me the two were planning to cut school. They walked out to the fence line next to the gym. He got over quickly, when he heard his friend yelling for help. His ring was caught on the top of the chain linked fence. As he tumbled over, the ring snapped his finger off. A staff member translated in Spanish what happened to his mother on the phone and where the family had to meet him at the University of California Los Angeles Medical Center.

Accidents can happen anywhere, and our students ran to us, the administrators, for help, when at school or in the community. We were there for them. Unfortunately, for this young man, UCLA Medical Center was not able to reattach his finger.

5

The Visitor

At another San Fernando Valley school, I had a conference scheduled one morning with a very special person. I didn't know it at the time. When the secretary came into my office, she was very excited, and with the commotion from the outer office, which I could hear, I sensed that something was different.

She told me a man was waiting to see me. So, I said, "Well, just send him in. He doesn't have to wait. I'm here and available." My secretary smiled shyly, and when she stepped back into the doorframe of my office with the gentleman, I looked up from my desk. Billy Dee Williams stood next to her, with his nephew behind him.

I couldn't believe it! I tried not to show my surprise. Here was this gorgeous man standing in my office. I remembered seeing his performances in "Lady Sings the Blues," "Mahogany" and "Star War" movies. What a handsome man, about 6 feet tall. Then I stood, which I would have done for any parent coming in and directed him and his nephew to seats with my heart beating wildly in my chest. My secretary closed the door as she left, confidence beaming on her face. She knew I was not prepared for this surprise.

I had received a call earlier in the morning from the nephew's mother whom I initially scheduled the conference with. She said she was not available, but she was sending her brother in her place. The conference was regarding a minor behavior issue in class. When I think back, many more Black boys were sent down for discipline that could have easily been handled by the teacher in the classroom. So, I had no problem talking with a representative of the family.

Mr. Williams was so gracious, very caring and supportive of his nephew and school expectations. At the end of the conference, he stood, nodded his head and extended his hand to me, while assuring me that his nephew would not be a problem anymore. I could hardly hear what he was saying, because his hands were smooth, warm, comforting. They felt really nice in the palm of my hand. I took a deep breath, before I dared to ask him. This was certainly out of the scope of my work, but I thought that I would take this opportunity to ask him anyway: Please sign an autograph for me and my daughter. I knew that Mia would get a big kick out of this story and Clarence too. He was a 'die hard' Star Wars fan. Mr. Williams willingly did so.

As he returned to the outer office, the secretary and clerks' eyes were glued on him, as well as the students, some of whom were service workers and other students sent down for a number of reasons, such as picking up attendance rosters, the morning bulletins, supplies and/ or they were being disciplined. As the students got up to greet the famous actor, I prepared a 'Back to Class' pass for his nephew, who was really a nice junior high school student.

***

I was proud of our students. They deserved so much more. Some of their lives were so difficult with people ready to harm them at every turn or they made poor decisions that could cost their lives. Even when it seemed adults lost hope, the students never gave up. But every now and then, I would catch a glimpse of their despair. Once, a lost notebook was turned in to me. As I flipped through the pages to find the student's name who owned it, I came across something deeply disturbing. There were pictures (mostly cut from magazines) of what the student wanted his funeral to include. This was a dark, yet powerful reminder of the depth of sorrow and hopelessness that he and so many of our children feel every day.

Our students were so resilient, and if given the resources and tools, they excelled despite the obstacles. Just to see students smile, with a reason to smile was uplifting. They were so talented. Their drama productions were like being in a theater in New York's Times Square. Senior English classroom debates on Shakespeare were another favorite that I would attend. Needless to say, their art exhibits were spectacular, dazzling with color, introspection and interest. The high schools that had automotive departments were another favorite. Students, with the help of the teacher, built engines from scrap, then started the engines to see which ones had the most power. My ears felt like they were exploding

21

from the noise generated. I was taken back to the Indiana Speedway 500 races, with every inch of my body at attention. Yes, these students had a lot to offer, if given the chance.

6

The Pinto

I was getting ready to leave the house one morning, when Clarence returned home from work, looking shaken and disheveled. What was he doing back here? I noticed smudges on his suit jacket and shirt, and Clarence is very particular about his clothing. Clarence took pride in his appearance. He always wore a suit to work. I asked, "What's wrong?" Then I said quietly, "What happened?" Between anger, fear, and hope, he shared that on his way to work in his sky-blue hatchback Ford Pinto, he had been pulled over by three or four police vehicles into a service station. They said that his car was stolen. I thought, 'Who would steal a Ford Pinto?' He was instructed to get out of his car, get his license and insurance papers, lie down with his face toward the ground, spread eagle on the asphalt surface, as they watched with guns and rifles pointed at him.

Clarence told me he did not open his glove compartment, not wanting to give these men any reason to report, "Dead on Arrival." He told the officers instead to get his papers. He continued, "Bev, I believed they were looking for any reason to kill me." My heart sank as I heard those words and knew well the truth in them. Easy prey! A Black man, alone, on his way to work, and this wasn't even Indiana. As an officer searched his vehicle, another contacted the dispatch unit. After lying on the ground for seemingly an hour, about fifteen minutes, he was told to go.

No apology and no, 'Sorry Sir.' Not even an offer of assistance with getting up from the greasy ground! To this day, that blue Pinto is long gone, but Clarence is still angry, and so am I.

***

The Rodney King verdict in 1992 sent a wave of hostility throughout the nation, followed by the rioting that we watched from our living room. Because our home is located in the hills, we could see fire from everywhere. Our Foreign Exchange Student daughter in Spain called to tell us she saw Crenshaw Boulevard burning on television. She was worried about us. Rodney King's simple yet emotionally complex question was, "Why can't we all just get along?"

When we returned to school (a different school) after the riots, National Guard greeted us in armored vans and those walking and or stationed at designated spots on tops of buildings had machine guns flanked across their camouflaged chests. No smiles, no words, like the Queen's Guards. I was nervous. Our high school was selected as a command post, because of its proximity to the freeway. Our students were so frightened, even the tough ones were careful. They had every reason to be. This was my first participation in what seemed like a police state, and it was scary. I did not like it.

As the Assistant Principal, I worked with many

outside agencies. The school's iconic gym was used in television commercials, because it was designed like an airplane hangar with large halfmoon windows exploding with natural light on each end. It was also used as a shelter for families displaced by the riots with resulting fires and the military. The gym floor was loaded with narrow framed metal beds and families huddled together with bags and boxes of Pampers seemingly everywhere.

7

Earthquake

The Northridge Earthquake exploded in 1994 with a magnitude of 6.7. Clarence and I were in San Diego Old Town with dear friends we met in Mexico City in the 1980's, when we were awakened early in the morning. We checked out of the hotel immediately, knowing our daughter was in the house alone in Los Angeles. On the way, we passed the San Onofre Nuclear Facility which always made me nervous, with concerns about leaks and deteriorating conditions. I had been in other earthquakes, but none this powerful. This earthquake brought back memories of my grandmother who was in the 1985 Mexico City 8.0 earthquake in which more than five thousand people died in that city alone. Trying to get the help of emergency organizations like the American Red Cross, and the Mexican Embassy was impossible. It took, at that time, almost a week for us to hear from her again. We were lucky. She survived.

At our home, our daughter recalled the early morning incident. She described being jolted, in an instant, out of a peaceful, quiet sleep into a thunderous and deafening hell that sounded like one hundred locomotives tearing through the center of our home. Each floorboard, skillfully laid decades earlier, retched and twisted violently as the house threatened to give way. She knew immediately it was an earthquake and tried to get out of bed but couldn't. The sheer force and power generated by the movement of the earth's tectonic plates propelled her back like a ragdoll against the headboard. With each thrust against the unforgiving surface, the muscles in her body tensed and convulsed. From deep within her, panic rose unconstrained as it tightened the muscles in her chest, forced its way up her throat and cut off her air way. She could feel her heart pounding uncontrollably and was conscious of the tension throbbing in her head. She heard glass shattering and other items falling throughout the house. However, she could not see from the morning darkness. Using all her energy, she rushed out as the bed and second floor steadied. Barefoot and frightened, she ran out of the house fearful that another jolt would come at any moment.

Outside, she was immediately startled by the cool water she felt between her toes. She paused for a moment, confused, and realized that water from the pool had spilled and splashed all over the backyard. Although she couldn't see if any damage had been done, she could hear the restlessness of the water and saw the early recognition of sunrise. Immediately she looked up and checked the power lines to be sure that they hadn't snapped. Across the city she could see flashes of blues, oranges and reds as power boxes blew and fires begin. She ran to the guest house on our property, where my childhood friend, Jason, lived. He was very concerned about his fiancé Janet who live 20 minutes away and insisted on checking on her. He refused to leave

Mia at the house alone, so they went together. As they pass the overpass of the 10 freeway, there was a sea of red brake lights and they knew what that meant. We later learned that one of the freeways had collapsed. Clarence and I made it back home that morning never really knowing how horrible our daughter's experience had been.

In addition to supporting my family and neighbors, as a school administrator I had to report to school to see the conditions after the earthquake, so decisions could be made regarding student safety. When I first stepped on campus with the school principal, it was eerie. I felt inside me a haunting presence. Nature had clearly rearranged the universe. The grounds were disturbed. There was a presence which left me feeling apprehensive, as if I was walking through a Halloween haunted house, expecting something to jump out at me.

When we opened the back door of the cafeteria, a small black bird, trapped from days before, flew across the ceiling and out the door. The blinds were closed, and a trace of sunlight reluctantly peeked through the vinyl slats. When we looked into the kitchen and adjoining storage room, I was speechless. Every enormous commercial refrigerator, stocked with food, was on the floor, like giant dominoes, collapsing onto each other.

Later, on our visit to the library, we had trouble opening the doors. Bending down, slipping our hands between the doors and the opening, we removed the books closest to the entrance. The doors slowly opened, as we pushed. It was shocking to see books EVERYWHERE! Every neatly stacked book from the shelves had become a missile, a projectile blasting off and about. All the shelves were empty, and a riverbed of books covered every inch of the floor in muted shades of reds, browns, gold and black book jackets. It looked like a rough cobblestone street in England. It was easy to think that this was a high school senior prank. I imagined the Librarian in tears after witnessing this fiasco. I sometimes thought she loved the books, and only tolerated the students as a necessary entity.

Each time I passed the section of the freeway that had fallen, I thought of the innocent people who were crushed with no chance of life.

***

So many things happened in our lives, both good and bad; but throughout all of this, I still had my brothers in my life. I heard from them all the time. As we got older, my brothers' sons came to spend the summer with my family and me. Later, my youngest sister's daughter spent the summers with us as well. Eddie spent time with me in Los Angeles for my birthdays and Christmas. Sometimes, he would bring his grandsons with him and we all had a good time. I am forever grateful.

Part 2

Hold On Kids!

I

New Beginnings

I grew up in "Jim Crow" Indianapolis, Indiana, beginning the winter of 1950, where my station in life was obvious, another Black child, but I didn't know that at the time. I stood next to my two older brothers, my anchors, at the airport, along with my mother.

I wasn't sure if this place, Indianapolis, Indiana, was going to work for me, nor if I would get used to having a physical father present in my life for the first time. I remember being four years old, and quite introspective. I didn't talk a lot, but I was a good listener, and I paid attention to my surroundings. At first the news of going to America was exciting. I thought the trip would be like driving through the Blue Ridge Mountains of Jamaica to visit relatives: plenty of children to play with, lots of homemade goodies to eat and people happy to see us; but this trip was not like that.

The thought of being on an airplane made my mother very happy with all the preparations, while leading to hopes for her family being together again. I knew I had to be with my mother. She needed me in her life, and I needed her and my two older brothers in mine. Norman was one year older than me and Orlando was a little over six years older than me. My oldest brother seemingly understood this new world, America, so I listened to him in anticipation.

But now with this uncaring wind slapping my face and making my eyes water when they opened the plane door, I was not so sure. I was perplexed by the Indiana winter: the sky was so gray, and the air was frosty cold. Where was the sunshine, the beautiful plants, and the flowers as there were in Jamaica? Many of the plants, I remembered, were large and luscious, bigger than my little body. This new land was barren. There were no leaves, no flowers, and ugly rough bark covering the trees that could scratch you.

What kind of world was this? Where were the mountains, the refreshing streams, the rolling hills, the grass? Yes, what happened to the grass? There was just dirt and concrete everywhere. What happened to the gentle breeze that softly kissed my cheek as I took a deep breath? Too many things were different!

***

I stood at the top of the plane's stairwell in my wool sweater seeing a man run towards us with arms loaded with coats. Orlando yelled, "…That's our father!" I just stared, so did Norman. Too cold to get excited about a man with coats! My mind could not make the connection. I was already an icicle. But Orlando's smile, with perfectly spaced teeth, was big enough for all of us. The excitement in his voice was contagious.

Before I knew it, my father had taken me into his arms and wrapped my new coat, leggings, hat and muff about me. But there was something in his movement, an abruptness, not kindness that I was expecting. When my mother went up to him, he handed her a coat and gently pushed her away from him. No smile!

It was, however, quite cold and maybe my father was just trying to get out of the weather, where we could all be comfortable. But there was definitely something amiss.

When I saw what my father did, I thought he was rude, and I made a mean face, which my father didn't see. I hoped my mother didn't see my face, either. I wouldn't want her to be hurt. My grandparent, Mammie and Papi, taught me that you always smiled and were gracious, even if you did not want to be, when meeting someone. This was the proper thing to do. My mother taught me that too; and these were my father's parents, so I know he was told the same.

My father, however, didn't smile at her, although he grinned profusely at me, us kids, while handing out coats, and helping us put them on. I sensed something was wrong. "I can feel it in my bones, child." That is what Mammie would say. I wasn't sure if she was talking about Mr. Arthur or Mr. Gout. She didn't smile when she talked about those pains. Mammie just rubbed some liniment on her knees. My aunties told her not to drink soda or eat Mackerel, one of her favorite dishes, which would help reduce the pain.

33

On Our Way

Well, this is the way our new life began. We flew TWA (Trans World Airlines) with tickets our father purchased for our family. I was so excited when the flight Attendant gave Norman and me our very own wings. They were plastic. She pinned it on my dress. My wings looked just like the one she wore on her uniform. She offered one to Orlando too, he looked at it, then said, "No thank you!" I'm sure he thought they were for kids, and he was not a child.

My mother sat next to the window. I sat next to her in the middle, and Norman had the aisle seat. Orlando's seat was on the aisle as well, but the row adjacent to us. He was elated. He was a big boy!

The cabin of the plane was very nice with navy blue comfortable leather seats. They distributed snacks first, then later served dinner in small beige containers. Food was good. I could have put the food tray in my little satchel, but there was no place to wash it.

I was surprised at the cloud formations. I didn't know clouds even had names, until Orlando shouted. "That's a cumulus nimbus cloud." As one of the flight attendants walked by, she replied, "That's right, young man!" Orlando was beaming, lost in the patterns. His American-made suit, although a little big, looked nice on him. He would be able to wear it again next year.

I looked out the windows when the clouds were beneath us. That really caught my attention, because it seemed so strange. We were flying above them. Remarkable! Like this puffy layer of cotton balls could hold the plane up. Then there was the sun, so intense, saturating the environment that I had to blink my eyes. I could see the sun's light span over the clouds, adding colors of the spectrum: soft blues, pinks, and reds extending as far as my eyes could see.

While my mother was napping, I asked Norman, "Why we have to leave Papi and Mammie (our grandparents). Why couldn't they come too?" Norman didn't even look at me, he just shrugged his shoulders hypnotized by the clouds that looked like scattered cotton balls pulled gently apart, then tossed about in the bright blue universe.

When we arrived in Indiana, everything was very different: The season, the sky, the penetrating cold. In a matter of hours, we went from hot, balmy and hopeful, to lost and lonely in a strange place.

Leaving the plane, we held the handrails of the portable stairwell and walked down to the tarmac. Immediately, the icy wind captured me in brittle coldness. I felt like a drip of an icicle firmly attached to the railing. I frowned as my chest muscles, blasted by the winter air, immediately constricted. I've never been that cold in my life. My eyes started to water as I tried not to fall grabbing my shoulders with my other arm, which threw my balance off.

I was wearing the cotton pink dress, my favorite color, which my Grandmother Phyllis made for me with neat little ruffles on the bottom and carried a store purchased cardigan sweater when we left 90° balmy weather in Jamaica. Now Orlando exclaimed, "Boy, it's 23 degrees out there." I thought at first, that he might pound on his chest, like he was a he-man, or something, but he didn't. I wondered where he got that number, then I saw the temperature flashing on the side of the airport building. That's how he knew.

He was really excited by this change in temperature. His face was pinkish red as he stood there with snow coming down, but I was perplexed. How did the temperature change so fast? I knew it was a big change in temperature, because I could feel it when they opened the door to the airplane. I tried subtracting the numbers in my head. Orlando tried to teach me this operation, he called it. But trying to carry the number in my head, I couldn't do it.

My eyes started to water again. I stuck my tongue out to taste those mysterious icy flakes sailing through the air. I saw Norman was doing the same thing, investigating the new world through our senses. What a strange treat this was coming from the sky. Snow... I heard of snow before and saw it on Christmas cards from America. This snow was really coming down fast though. When it hit the ground, some of it melted and others formed little patches of sleet, a combination of ice and snow. That was another new word.

Through insipid eyes, I could barely see the man coming forth with the coats, but Orlando yelled with exhilaration, "There he is! That's our Father." Other than my mother, Orlando was the only one of my father's children who could identify him.

He was wearing a full-length camel colored cashmere coat. That's what my older brother called it, a wool felt brimmed hat, low on his brow, covering most of his round brown face.

"That's our father," Orlando yelled again with glee. I recognized the smile in my brother's voice. He was happy. Our father came to get us. He did not forget us.

I couldn't remember what he brought my brothers, but in my mind, they were two padded car coats, boxy like a Peacoat; but what he brought me, I will never forget.

It was an oxblood wool coat with matching padded leggings, that were too long, but my father swiftly rolled them up, tucked my dress in the waist, and folded the sleeves into the hollow chamber of the coat's arms. Then he placed a white rabbit fur hat, fully lined, snuggly on my head, with flaps that covered my ears, and tied the hat under my chin, a little too tightly, but I could loosen it later.

For my hands, he held a white matching fur muff. My

eyes widened. 'Could this be mine,' I questioned? Inside of the muff was thick padding. However, this is what I could not believe: the muff had the lovely face of a white doll. My other dolls were black rag dolls that Mammie and my aunties handmade for me from scraps of leftover fabric. I like them too.

This white doll with a gentle molded plastic face, was, however, definitely store bought. The doll had pink cotton candy-like cheeks, and big brown eyes. I was in awe!

I really could not enjoy her at the time, because my father was in such a big rush, something about his car had to be moved.

Our family walked carefully through the slush on the runway. My father was ahead of us, trying to get to his car. We were really the last passengers off the plane, when I looked back and saw flight attendants behind us. I finally had to skip to keep up. My patent-leather shoes were sliding back and forth in the new red galoshes my father also bought me.

Beginning to feel hot, with moisture creeping across my forehead, I took my hands out of my muff, loosened the hat and carried it while in the airport, where it was warm. I kept an eye on my father, and Orlando kept an eye on me, and waited for me to catch up. I knew he would. My mother was not far behind me; but I knew that Orlando would be there. He was my "Big Brother."

***

As I said earlier, this was not the usual family gathering on a day trip. In fact this journey to Indianapolis, Indiana was really different. We were initially so excited: being on an airplane, wearing special clothes for the occasion, getting wings from the flight attendant, seeing clouds up so close, and needless to say, getting my warm coat, white fur hat with the matching muff and beautiful doll in the center. This should have been an exciting day!

However, no one came to greet us at the airport: no children or cousins, no neighbors. Not even the sun came out to greet us! We were truly alone in our own little world for the first time, and I did not like it. I wanted to go back to Jamaica to my grandparents, aunts and uncles. I felt really sad. I was worried my mother was sad also. The gentle face of my doll muff, smiling into my eyes, however, gave me just a little hope, as I checked quickly for Norman and Orlando.

3

Disappointment

That first winter was a major disappointment for my mother and us children, following her lead. We were constantly moving, because our mother said our father could not find rental housing that accepted children. So, he told the landlord that the place was only for himself and his wife, which was never true. When the owners realized there were three children in the house, even though we were very quiet, really, we were, we still had to move. At that time, there were not laws that protected the housing rights of children in Indianapolis; and as a youngster, I would not have known that anyway; and I don't think that my mother understood this law either.

It was discrimination against families. Discrimination was a word I learned much later, but I knew early it meant, "I was not wanted." My mother was also new to Indianapolis, so she didn't know about discrimination either, but she learned. America was '...the land of the free, and the home of the brave.' My mother repeated these words from the "Star Spangled Banner," which were truly part of what she believed; but there was a question in my mind. It appeared to me that America was for certain people, and maybe my family was not included among them.

My father selected Indianapolis, Indiana, because he was a divinity student at Butler University. So, in addition to his two jobs, he also went to school a couple of nights a week. He prepared sermons, which he practiced religiously, and recorded on a reel-to-reel machine. I was mesmerized seeing those two big wheels slowly turning. His voice sounded weird to me on that machine and his Jamaican accent was really strong. One of his favorite biblical quotes was, "*Silver and gold, have I none, but such as I have, give I thee, in the name of Jesus Christ, arise and walk....*"

However, it was my father we blamed for our misery. After all, he brought us to America and paid for our tickets, so it was entirely his fault. We never smiled at him, nor did we laugh at his little jokes. I did not sit on his lap and listen to accounts of his day, nor he mine. We were angry with him. Just what was he planning? Our mother was suspicious and so were we. What if he wasn't the man my mother thought he was? What if he was an imposter? Orlando explained to me what an imposter was. So, I was suspicious of our father too.

Our father was the man who said to our mother, when she was seventeen, "You are a lily in a stagnant pool, and I am going to pluck you right out of there," referring to the life my mother lived with our angry grandmother. That's the man we wanted. My mother stared into the ceiling, like she was looking into the sky or something, as she reflected and repeated my father's words while wiping moisture from her forehead and tears from her eyes. "You are a lily in a stagnant pool…," remembering that life, while truly believing having a mother in her life would have made everything better. It had not. But my mother really believed and imbued, 'God answers prayer. Be patient!' Although during this time, I wondered if the answer she received was the one she wanted.

The family did, however, (no matter how mad we were with our father), eat the food he brought home, meats and all, some prepared at the Marriot Hotel where he worked and would bring home leftovers; other packaged items from the grocery included bread, muffins, shredded wheat and corn flake cereals; raisin buns with sticky white frosting; Oreo and oatmeal cookies; Hostess Twinkies; and the milk, which he left on the freezing back porch overnight, for our breakfast the next day. We waited for the milk to thaw with Orlando's help in the mornings.

Orlando added a little water to the milk, and then he shook and shook, making sure the lid did not come off, until it became slushy, like a shake. It was really good that way. We started to Americanize through foods that were not necessarily dissimilar, but prepared differently; yet tasty: American fried chicken – nothing like Jamaican fried chicken (not crispy); BBQ ribs – don't remember that taste, but maybe closer to jerk meats; donuts – no donuts; cakes with frostings - we ate spice buns and rum cakes, no frosting other than a little cinnamon with melted brown sugar; Hershey chocolates – our chocolates didn't come in paper – but we drank chocolate tea; ice-cream – America, definitely, was the best, because it was frozen.

My brothers would place their hands over their tummies and push their bellies way out, laughing and Orlando would say, "Boy, this is real good." Norman would follow with, "Sure is! Real Good," Norman repeated as Orlando added more Hershey Chocolate syrup to their milk. I was surprised how big they could make their tummies stick out. I could not do my stomach like that.

During the days when my father went to work, my mother sat at the table and mostly cried. We children sat with her, just wanting to be near her. She was our remembrance of family.

I was thin and cold, so I wiggled my fingers inside my muff and my toes inside my shoes, as Orlando told me to, while I tried to concentrate on what my mother was saying. We wore our winter coats in the house, because there was no heat. Before our father left for work, he started a fire in the fireplace, and Orlando kept it going during the day.

My mother mumbled over and over through swells of tears spilling on to her red, puffy face. "Why would he deny having children, my children, our children? Why would he do that?" At first, it was not clear to me why my mother was so upset. Even if my father said that, we were still right here, and he had to feed us. Right? But she repeated this question every day. It certainly weighed heavily on her heart.

43

At these times, our eyes and hearts were focused on our mother. She was unhappy, so we were unhappy too. Our father made us all unhappy. We, too, wanted to know why he did this?

"He (*our father*) spent years saving money and getting sponsors for us," my mother said. "Why, if he was going to deny his children even existed? None of this makes any sense," our mother questioned out loud, (not really talking to us), just tripping over the meaning of my father's actions in her heart.

Later, I asked Orlando, "What's a sponsor?"

He answered proudly as if he was reciting a reading in a classroom. "Sponsors are citizens of the United States who are in good standing. They do everything right. So, the government allows them to stand up for us. In other words, they believe we will make good citizens too."

'He was so smart,' my big brother, I thought. 'He knew so many things, could fix anything; so resourceful, and he knew where to get everything.' America seemed just the right fit for him.

***

Ironically, Orlando was the only one of us three children huddled at the airport in December of 1950, who never got his

American citizenship. I was eleven years old, when we were scheduled to meet at the immigration office. My mother had to take classes; but as children, we did not, because we attended American schools. In a capacity filled auditorium of an Indiana state office building, my mother, brother Norman, and I stood in front of the hundreds of metal folding chairs. The chairs in the front were empty. On that cold day in March 1958, we recited the Pledge of Allegiance to the flag of the United States of America in unison with other people, while I looked frantically for Orlando, who was now sixteen. I watched my mother's eyes as she searched the room for him too. She looked worried.

When I turned to look, I saw my father, smiling that crooked grin, in the middle row of the chairs; but my older brother was not with him. "Where was he?" I never knew why he didn't show up. Later, when I asked Orlando, he evaded my question, chuckling instead. Then said, "It's no big deal."

But it was to me, a really 'big deal.' I didn't want him to get deported if something happened. That's what they did to immigrants who were not naturalized citizens. They told us that in school. I had never been in America without my big brother and I did not want it to change. My older brother, however, remained a Jamaican national until his death in 1999 of heart disease, never fully participating in the American dream our father envisioned for us with voting rights, property rights, human rights and religious freedoms.

***

Orlando, craftily, created his own life in America. Ironically, maybe his life was the American dream. He was artistically talented without training, and his mechanical abilities surpassed any kid I knew. He used his God-given talents. He could fix anything. He had bicycles in the garage and a couple of cars lined up in the alley, where friends, neighbors, all by word of mouth, parked and waited their turns. Other guys came by just to be around him. He had a great sense of humor. It was like an entertainment show. He was quick witted and before you could think of a response, people were already laughing at some brash comments Orlando made. I watched him from the alley gate. He stood confidently, like a straight man in a comedy routine. He did not want his little sister to be in the alley, unless other neighborhood girls were around, playing kickball, or hopscotch.

Orlando was brilliant in so many ways, but our father rarely saw those gifts in him. Generally, his school grades were low. He just was not interested in school. When my father tutored him, he hit Orlando on the knuckles with a ruler, and talked really cross to him. They did not get along at all; but my father really did not get along with any of us. I think that my brother decided anything my father did well, he would not do. But there were things he was great at: fixing cars and bicycles, landscaping, plants, caring for animals – mending broken wings and legs - and returning them to nature. He was patient and kind.

He could also fix anything in the house, a broken window - before our parents got home, the washing machine, gas stove, and he was an excellent cook, specializing in savory sauces with just the right taste of garlic and other seasonings.

Orlando was offered a General Motors Scholarship and job training after high school, but he blew it, not realizing he had to actually graduate from high school first.   Instead, he married a girl from another high school, and his life changed, tumbled over with accidents, family and health issues; but he never lost his smile, except sometimes when he looked vacantly at his children, at a loss about their future. With me however, he was always joking and confident.

4

Peak of Winter

Our family's arrival in America in the peak of winter posed major problems; and because my father did not acknowledge his children, we sat bundled and huddled in the houses he rented, in the heavy coats he bought for us, wearing layers of clothing my mother packed from Jamaica, with no heat, no lights, and only running water. Our father worked two jobs, the Marriott Hotel and at the church where he supervised the recreational activities, where he kept warm. Some evenings, we went with our father to the church, but the gym was cold too as I sat on the wooden bench, wrapped like a snowman. My father didn't believe girls should run up and down a basketball court. It was not a lady-like thing for girls to do. My brothers played, and I watched them; toyed with my muff doll. I wiggled my toes inside my shoes and my fingers inside my muff, swinging my thin legs back and forth, while trying desperately not to think of the cold.

At night, my father lit candles in the rooms we used. It seemed creepy to me, with the flame casting wiggling figures on the walls. However, in the parlor, there was a kerosene lamp that had a plastic revolving shade with pictures of a cabin in the countryside, waterfalls and a train. As the lamp heated up, the shade revolved faster and faster around the base, casting silhouettes from the lamp's shade about the room. It was so interesting, and calming, capturing my attention as I sat for an hour or so. A scenic tour of this new world included trains moved slowly around the room, until the kerosene was gone.

Every evening, the movements with its lights and shadows fascinated me, and my eyes darted around the room in anticipation. I sat by myself, but I was real happy. The room turned into this 'Merry-go-round' of amusement, which captivated me. One evening I had gotten up to carefully examine the lamp's base that propelled the shade's images about the room. When the shade slowed or the kerosene and or the wick went out, the movement of the figures halted.

I was so excited I got too close to the opaque kerosene container and burned my left arm before I even knew it. My arm ached for more than a week, with the burn swelling in a bubbly sick whitish color. I put Vaseline on my burn and used a paper napkin so my injury would not stick to my clothing. I did not say anything to my mother or brothers. My suffering was in silence, but most of the time, my mind was occupied with new aspects of living in America, so I hardly felt anything. Presently, I can't see the scar from that accident any longer, but my mind knows exactly where it was.

***

In the daytime, I blew my breath into the air, and watched as warm vapors escaped my lips. But blowing onto the glass was a fun thing to do, while making patterns on the window of the door with my fingers. I kissed the glass just slightly with dry lips, so my mouth would not stick to the surface, because that hurt. With moist lips when I tried to peal my skin away, tiny slivers of my lips with blood on it, stuck to the glass. However, an imprint of my lips on the window would appear before me. Sometimes, I blew my breath into my hands to warm them up. I remember, my mother cleaning the window with Windex a lot. I saw streams of heated air escaping from the mouths of my brothers and mother when they talked. We all looked like little hot teapots.

***

That first year, for Christmas, the church my father attended gave us a holiday gift basket, part of their missionary program -a frozen turkey, Brown n' Serve rolls, canned yams, corn, and red and green peppermint candies wrapped in clear plastic with twisted ends. My father, a very proud man, accepted the gift basket, but did not tell these people we had no gas for cooking, no lights and no heat. I guess he was too proud to mention those facts.

When my mother saw the gift basket, she couldn't even say, 'Thank you.' She just jumped up, sobbing, running to their bedroom. My father stood there with the basket in his hand, looking lost, as his eyes followed her. We children looked at him; and again, immediately connected him to our mother's unhappiness. Initially, I did not understand why my mother was so upset. The basket, wrapped in clear cellophane paper, with a bright red velvet ribbon, looked really nice to me. I would have smiled and been very happy, if I had not seen my mother's reaction.

The next day, a lady from the church stopped by. The lady asked my mother if our family liked the gift. After learning our circumstances, she arranged for the frozen turkey, now slightly defrosted, to be cooked at another location along with the trimmings for our Sunday dinner. I thought that was really great and wondered why my father did not think of it.

I started thinking then that my father was a coward; or at least, he was pretending to be something he was not.

That's what my older brother said. "He's just prancing around, like a rooster, before the hens." I remembered the rooster running around in the backyard of my grandparents' home in Jamaica, with white chickens in the coup. I stayed away from the speckled brown, black and white feathered cock, because this bird was really mean. He pecked you, fast and quick; and if you didn't move pronto, he pecked you again. I ran from that rooster. I learned quickly!

***

My brothers and I walked the street in the afternoon feeling the warmth of the sun, although we could not see it. It was cold, but we had each other, laughing and talking along the way. It was like being on the dirt paths in Jamaica, going to the Parish or going to play with other children. Orlando had so much to tell us, so many insights. It was comfortable. I

51

studied the trees, particularly the bark, as I listened to him. There were not trees like this in Jamaica, with no leaves, no fruit. Yet, I found them interesting. I could see golden colored sap frozen in the crevices. Orlando said these were Maple trees, and people made syrup from the sap. He said simple ways of catching the sap had developed over time, which they used for meals, poured over pancakes. He saw pictures in a library book. I wondered how he knew so much.

My brothers were not in school at the time, because we did not have a permanent address. During the day, it was nice to have them with me. My mother was layered in her pink chenille bathrobe with bumpy rolls of little cotton balls stitched to the surface. The robe just barely touched the floor; a full-length slip; an island-patterned dress; and the mutton coat my father bought her at the airport rested on her shoulders. She sat like an abominable snowman at the dining table with a crumpled white handkerchief in her hand day after day, bloated face and swollen eyes, lonely. She told Orlando what she wanted, and he gave Norman and me her instructions.

The next week, with arrangements my father made with the minister at the church, we moved in with a retired husband, and his homemaker wife, who were members of the church. Their children were grown and out of the house. The wife was very kind. She had smooth dark brown skin, short cut silky-silver hair, a slim figure, and wore lovely clothes. She wasn't tall, nor her husband, but had a very comfortable voice. She didn't mind us being around: in fact, she liked children. She talked and laughed with me, made me feel relaxed. This temporary living arrangement went on until my father found another possibility.

5

The Nativity

In 1951, my youngest brother, Eddie, was born in September. The church was planning its annual Nativity Scene production in December, and the Reverend asked my mother to play the role of Mary and my little brother, Baby Jesus, in the manger. My mother agreed. I sat in the church's multipurpose auditorium/gymnasium that evening among a full crowd watching my mother and baby brother in the manger scene. The audience, I am sure, was there for all their wonderful memories of the Nativity. It was Christmas time after all. I was there for my mother and baby brother.

It was surprising to me how Eddie never cried or moved his head. When my mother lifted him from the manger and his eyes were fixed on her, he never uttered a word. I was in awe! It was as if my baby brother knew he was playing a special role.

Many of the church people thought baby Jesus was a doll, until a hush fell over the audience when they saw my brother move and turn his head toward the spotlight which highlighted them on stage. My mother wore the border of a white sheet folded and clipped to her hair, and the remaining fabric draped across her body. The three wise men were in the scene as well. It was most impressive. I was inspired. It was, after all, 'My mother' and 'My baby brother.' The exit lights were barely noticeable in the dark auditorium.

After the production, I followed other members to the stage. I waited below as adults walked up the stage steps to the manger, thanking my mother for a beautiful presentation. She smiled demurely, while accepting their accolades. I watched and listened, proud again of them both. Needless to say, my father was ecstatic.

My father had the biggest smile, somewhat crooked on his round face. He accepted compliments from the minister (Pastor, they called him), and assistant ministers. You would have thought my father was in the production. In Jamaica, we called the Anglican minister, "Father." Here in the Baptist church, the names were different.

My father worked at the Baptist church two evenings a week and on Saturdays, supervising the activities of the young people in the gym for which he was paid.

***

The next year, Orlando played the role of one of the wise men, Balthazar. By that time however, my youngest brother Eddie, who played baby Jesus the year before, was running around. My baby brother was too active for the role now, baby Jesus was again a doll.

6

Ronnie

A year later, our family, now four children moved again. Our father was able to get more permanent housing for us in a home that was owned and occupied by an elderly lady who could not walk and was blind. Her name was Mrs. Day. She occupied the living room as her bedroom. A caretaker, Pauline, who came every day to fix her food, change her sheets, rotate her body and tend to her toileting. There was a downstairs bathroom for Mrs. Day, and the one upstairs was for our family. The rooms of the house, with the exception of the living room Mrs. Day occupied, included three bedrooms upstairs, and a dining room downstairs rented to my father and the backyard, loaded with dandelion greens, which Pauline picked from the yard and cooked. The greens were too strong for me, "yukky!" However, my mother and Orlando liked them. Our family had more space in this rented house. We were happy, I suppose. Although no one ever asked me; but we could make friends.

Orlando went everywhere in the new neighborhood on his bicycle. I don't know how he got that bicycle, maybe he traded services for it. He introduced Norman and me to Ronnie, who lived across the street. My older brother was friendly with Ronnie's two older brothers, and they worked on bicycles together, placing lights all over them. Ronnie and

I were probably the same age, but he was a little chubby, and looked older than me because I was so thin. He had thick black wavy hair, really pretty for a boy, and long eyelashes, which curled. The little guy was gorgeous. I had none of these features. I was 'plain Jane' and thin, with fine hair as well. A ribbon couldn't stay in place, so my mother plaited my hair every morning with several small braids about my head. I believe that she thought my hair would grow out that way.

***

Ronnie's house was on a sloping hill across the street from us. You walked up about five steps to get to the landing, and probably three or four more steps to the front door in the built-in screened porch. Two shiny black Cadillac limos were parked in front of his home every day. I sometimes waved to his father, or his pretty mother, who looked like a movie star with long flowing black shiny hair down her back, wearing bright red lipstick, getting into one of the limousines. The next year, I was surprised to see his mother in a curly bob cut. She looked cute that way too, but I wondered what she did with all that long hair. Did they use it to make hair for someone who didn't have any or maybe for dolls? It would have been nice if they stitched it up and then I could have pinned it to my braids. I could then shake my head about while watching the tresses fly through the air attached to my braids.

Ronnie had more toys than anyone I knew. Toys filled every inch of his room – which he had to himself, and the toys were

VERY EXPENSIVE. I know this, because our toys were small plastic ones, which broke easily; and my father bought them at the grocery store, other than the little inch thumb metal cars he also bought for my brothers there. Ronnie let Norman and me play with his fancy bright yellow steel Tonka trucks, late model metal cars of all brands, like his red Cadillac convertible, turquoise-blue Thunderbird, his Volkswagen Beetle, as well as other toy planes and ships, in shades of gray, on the shelves.

It seemed like he got a new Schwinn bike every year for Christmas or his birthday, with reflector lights, detailed paints with hand-rubbed luster. He let Norman ride any bike he was not riding and offered a bike to me too. However, I chose not to ride after trying it once, because boy bicycles were too uncomfortable with that bar that hit my 'puum puum,' I mean my private parts. I was not tall enough to extend above the bar. He and my brother Norman were taller, so they were fine. I wished my father would buy me a bike for girls. A couple of years later, my father did buy me a bright red fire truck from Sears, with white stripes and two wooden ladders on each side. Norman and I used the ladders as walking stilts. My brothers would take turns pushing me in my little truck, so I could go faster. But I could ride it by myself, by pumping the paddle wheels beneath the shiny red hood.

Ronnie's family garage looked like a bicycle store. I thought that was why the black Cadillac limos were always parked in front; but I suppose the limos were really too long to fit into the garage. He also had a scooter and a red wagon which he and my brother pulled me in sometimes. They were kept in the garage.

Ronnie was kind of soft and pudgy 'baby fat,' the kids would say, with skin like creamy vanilla ice cream. He was 'real' nice. His older brothers teased him a lot (as Orlando teased Norman, endlessly), so Ronnie cried often; but when his brothers were gone, he was a lot of fun. I thought his family was rich, but what did I know. It was, however, clear to me Ronnie had lots of good stuff.

7

Mrs. Day

My mother shared the kitchen with Pauline, Mrs. Day's caretaker. She arrived daily at 7:00 in the morning and left about 7:00 p.m. in the evening. Pauline taught her how to make many American southern dishes. During the spring and summer, I watched Pauline dig dandelion greens from the backyard, and prepare them for dinner. I enjoyed blowing the hairy white seed balls of the dandelion, which looked like a feathery sucker. I chased my brothers with them, as I took a breath and blew the seeds at them. They would pretend they could not get away. Sometimes, my brothers would blow the seed at me, and then I would run as fast as I could. I also picked the yellow daisies and made bouquets for my mother. I didn't know the health virtues of dandelions, but I knew they tasted nasty. My mother was always saying, "Eat your vegetables," but she didn't make me eat those.

Mrs. Day's room was always dark, and it scared me at first. I knew it did not matter to her, because she could not see anyway; but I wondered how she could live her life in a bed each and every day, wearing a cotton or nylon nightgown. Periodically, she listened to Fur Elise and Liebestraum on a record player, which Pauline played for her.

Sometimes I sat in her room and listened too, with my eyes closed, imagining how Mrs. Day might feel, with random thoughts running through her mind. What did she think about? What were her memories? Were they good ones or sad ones? I never saw her cry like my mother did. She never seemed angry or even disappointed. How did she manage that? Later I thought maybe she was medicated, but I would not have known it at the time.

The music, however, was so compelling, I sometimes got lost in its cadences and its enriching melodies. At times, I didn't even remember I was with Mrs. Day. I dozed off into a dreamy world, where possibilities were endless.

"You there, child?" Mrs. Day spoke politely. She swallowed with a clacking sound in the back of her throat.

I opened my eyes and looked at Mrs. Day's head cradled in the pillow, extended just above a short narrow neck. She looked doll-like.

"Oh yes, Mrs. Day," I said as I eased myself up in the chair and adjusted my eyes to the sunlight in the room. "Who's playing the piano?" I asked as my mind returned to the present.

"It's a recording by Arthur Rubinstein, Dear," she said in a high voice, swallowed again, a gurgling sound in her throat like spit switching along a flashtube, as she moved her head

61

in the direction of my voice. "He is quite a pianist and is well known all over the world."

"People pay him to play the piano?" I asked, thinking that was pretty remarkable.

"They sure do Dear," she swallowed again and clicked something in her throat. "They sure do." She took another breath, followed quickly by a gurgling sound.

***

Before I knew it, Mrs. Day drifted back into a deep sleep. I suppose it was impossible to tell when it was night, so sleep consumed her all the time.

This sweet old lady with nothing else to do, trapped in a body that had long ago given up. Ironically, Mrs. Day had a nice slim body, cocoa brown, tall with long slender legs. How was it that this body was not interested in her life? Why was that? She had no visitors, yet I vaguely remember a young couple who came to see her on a Sunday afternoon. Don't recall them ever coming back, at least not when my family was there. I thought it was possibly a daughter with a husband. But no one told me. Pauline never said anything. Mrs. Day was dressed in a floral print hostess gown with matching robe – shiny polyester. It was lovely. I wanted to touch it. Pauline prepared snacks for the visitors: sliced cheeses, crackers, chicken wings, and watermelon. Mrs. Day's family nor ours ever entertained anyone in the house. So, it was a special day.

On other days, Pauline turned the knob of the small radio sitting on the bottom shelf of Mrs. Day's mahogany bedside table. Mrs. Day listened to the news all the time, and Orson Welles with his deep voice was one of her favorites, as well. Mr. Welles seemed mysterious to me, so I was a little frightened by his stories. They seemed dark, scary and I thought the ending was not going to be good. Mrs. Day also loved Groucho Marx, and she laughed. Sometimes, her laughing led to coughing, but she laughed anyway.

Pauline poked her head in. I was glad to see her, because I thought Mrs. Day was choking and she couldn't stop. "You alright?" she asked.

Sometimes I thought she would die right there on the spot, which scared me. I would have to run for help, but it never happened.

I laughed nervously too as I imagined Groucho with his bushy eyebrows and crazy eyeglasses. I had seen him on our neighbor's RCA Victor television set.

My mother told me Mrs. Day was paralyzed from a stroke and later blinded by diabetes. She could move her arms, head, her eyes and talk. However, deep swallows punctuated her speech with her own set of circulating pumps with fluids running back and forth in her throat. Yet Mrs. Day never seemed bitter. I'd be really mad, if I couldn't go out to play – or if my skinny legs could not carry me to places I wanted to go. But never Mrs. Day! She somehow reconciled her life to a limb of petrified wood in a forest, still valuable however, with her eyes open to observe all around her. She was always pleasant, but totally dependent on Pauline.

Pauline was tall, on the plump side, similar yellow brown coloring as my mother; and she was so nice. She never yelled or looked angry. I thought Pauline was probably in her thirties, with smooth soft skin. I watched as she worked and saw the light reflect moisture off her sleeveless shoulders. She wore her hair pulled back in a tiny ponytail, more like a pigtail with a scarf tied around the nape of her head. Pauline never mentioned having any children or a husband. Therefore, I never asked. They always told us kids, "Stay out of grown folks' business."

When I spent a little time with Mrs. Day, Pauline always opened the drapes, and a profusion of light flooded the room as prisms of color danced about the walls. Mrs. Day was always glad when I came in to talk to her. Her face would light up. Her eyes wide open, though she could not see. I thought that was odd. I wasn't frightened with the daylight coming in. Otherwise, her room was pitch black with drapes and blinds closed against the windows. Not sure why that was necessary. Maybe, it had to do with circadian or nocturnal rhythms, something like that, Orlando said; but I didn't know what it meant.

Ms. Day never asked to feel my face, like in Helen Keller's life story; but she did ask one day, "How tall are you, Dear?" I did not know, so she said, "Come here, child," she paused, clicking sounds in the back of her throat, "and let me check."

"Come closer, Dear," she said and swallowed, clicking sounds from her throat again. "Bend towards me." Her throat made the sound again, and she took another breath.

I don't know if she could feel the change in the air or what. How could she tell how tall I was? But she seemed satisfied with this gesture.

"Do you have enough light Dear?" She swallowed again.

"Oh yes, Mrs. Day," I said. "Plenty! I can see good!"

"Good girl," she said, smiling followed by a clicking swallow. She took a big breath, "No need for you to be sitting in the dark with an old gizzard like me." She took another breath. "What did you do today?"

"I played with Ronnie and Norman," I told her.

"Those little boys can be a little rough, so you be careful."

"Yes, Mrs. Day, I will."

But, I had so many things to ask her. My questions spilled out of my mouth, like a fountain. They were in my mind for so long, that I had to get them out. "What happened to your legs? Why can't you walk? How is it that you can blink your eyes, but you can't see? How long have you been blind? Did it happen all at once, or just one day, Kaboom! And everything went black!"

"Hold on Darling!" Mrs. Day sounded a little winded, took a deep breath.

I realized then I was asking too many questions, too fast.

"It is nice of you to come and talk to an old lady." She stopped. "No one talks to me much anymore, but Pauline. It's a delight for me to answer your questions." She swallowed, clacking sound in her throat.

I saw Pauline in the doorway. She looked concerned.

"By the way, how is your mother?" Mrs. Day swallowed again, seemingly calmer.

I realized I was breathing fast. So, I took a deep breath. "Oh, she will talk to you later. She's with my baby brother. She said I should not bother you too much."

"You are never a bother, child." She swallowed, taking her time as she searched the room with her eyes, but I knew she could not see. "You bring me life." Then she smiled as she turned her head towards the sound of my voice.

"Now let me see Dear," Mrs. Day laughed; because she knew she could not see. I chuckled too. "One day, a long time ago, I was heading to my bedroom," she swallowed. "I wasn't rushing or anything, when I felt like a bolt of lightning passing through my head." It sounded scary to me! I was always frightened when those big summer storms hit, with giant bolts of lightning across the sky. She paused. "I grabbed my head," she swallowed again, with a clicking noise, and I could imagine her grabbing her head, just as if I was there with her. She continued, "because, I was in so much pain. I must have fallen on the steps."

Mrs. Day paused, "and hit my head, because I passed out. When I woke up," she made a gurgling sound, "everything was different. The room was stark white, white sheets, white pillowcases, people around me in white," she swallowed again, followed by a clicking noise. "A doctor, some nurses, you know, Dear. I was in a hospital." She waited.

Pauline stepped closer to the bed.

"That was when I realized my legs did not work." Mrs. Day swallowed hard again. "I was really frightened, but no one I knew was there, but faintly I saw other patients in cubicles throughout the ward." She took a deep breath. "I supposed they were like me (gurgle sound). A young white doctor came over to my bedside." She swallowed. "He looked at me intensely."

"You awake?" he asked. "He went on to tell me I had a stroke." She made a sound in the back of her throat again.

"It was touch and go for a while," the doctor continued, "but we thought that there was still a chance to get your legs working again with therapy." Mrs. Day rested again, I smiled at this good news, but she couldn't see me.

"But we couldn't afford it Dear, - a convalescent home - I mean," she swallowed. "That's what he recommended. It is where they have all these people trained to help you walk again."

Pauline appeared a little anxious. I could see concern in her face.

"So, the hospital released me, and I went home." She waited. I hoped she was not getting too tired. Taking a series of short breaths, Mrs. Day continued. "My family helped me move my legs each day. They massaged them good, use Ben Gay ointment, but I never walked again." She looked deflated as her chest sunk into the bed. "I was sad about it." "Pauline still rubs my legs with liniment." Mrs. Day looked like she was going to cry.

She struggled momentarily with the muscles in her jaws. I could see them tense, then relax. I stared into Mrs. Day's eyes. They were open. The white parts were a little yellow - brownish color, but her lenses were covered with a thickened bluish lump. Then her eyelids slowly closed, like brown crinkled curtains.

Pauline gestured for me to leave. I was glad to go. I didn't want Mrs. Day to die while talking to me.

Periodically, over the next week or so, I stopped by Mrs. Day's room before I went out to play. She was sleep.

Then one day, I stood in the doorway and waited as I noticed Pauline leaving with Mrs. Day's white wash-up basin. She said encouragingly, "Come in child," swallowed, then continued. "What's on that mind of yours?"

I thought it was amazing how Mrs. Day could sense my presence.

"Well," I hesitated, wondering if I should really say what was on my mind.

"Spill it out," Mrs. Day said somewhat gaily.

I wasn't sure I should 'spill it out,' especially after last week when my questions made Mrs. Day so sad.

But she was asking me, so I took a gentle breath and said a little shyly, "I just want to ask one more thing." My eyes glued to the floor. My hands joined behind my back. I waited for permission.

"Go on child," Mrs. Day said, as I heard her take a deep breath.

I took a breath too. "Oh, Mrs. Day, why couldn't they pay for it? It's not fair, just not fair!" My heart started racing as I thought about what happened to this sweet old lady.

"Well Dear, many things aren't fair," she swallowed. I watched her Adam's apple move up and down in her throat. "And we didn't have insurance; but managed somehow." She paused. "A couple of years later, I lost my eyesight."

"Oh Mrs. Day. That is really not fair, I mean really not." I wanted to scream out at the world, at God, at the doctor, but what was the use? Mrs. Day would still lie here entombed in her body.

***

I still remember Mrs. Day and see her talking with my mother in that darkened room. Sometimes, my mother had my baby brother, Eddie, with her. It made Mrs. Day very happy.

Mrs. Day was smart. I knew she had gone to school, because she sounded like the teachers, I had in Bible school and my Kindergarten, knowledgeable and soft-spoken.

When I think back, Mrs. Day was reduced to a fraction of the physical person she was; but the woman I met as a child – was absolutely incredible! We called her Mrs. Day, so I assumed that there was a Mr. Day who was no longer alive. I never asked her, not wanting to bring up any more bad memories. I believed that she was consumed by memories, because what else did she have? What was the point in looking to the future? I, on the other hand, looked forward to playing with friends, riding bikes, chasing my brothers, going to school; but Mrs. Day's life was exactly the same each day. There was nothing for her to look forward to, other than, of course, another day she could not recognize.

Our family moved out of Mrs. Day's home into our first home where my parents actually had a mortgage and were no longer renters. My mother borrowed $1000.00 from the doctor she worked for to make the down payment. It was at this time my mother told me Pauline called to say that Mrs. Day died peacefully in her sleep. She lived, as she had died, tranquilly, in complete harmony with her life. I said a little silent prayer for Mrs. Day. I never saw her again; but somehow, I see her still.

8

Childhood Fear

By the age of six, I had already experienced more than most of my contemporaries in America. My mother, brothers and I, left behind everything familiar to us in Jamaica, BWI, and moved to America to connect with our father and establish new roots. The transition was difficult for our family. Yet along the way, we eventually became part of a church family, developed new relationships, bought a new home and made life-long connections in our new neighborhood. As kids, life in America proved to bring a host of new and unforgettable experiences

***

When we were little kids, Norman was afraid of a few natural and unnatural phenomenon, like most kids. However, I never knew anyone other than Norman who was afraid of his shadow, which I could not understand. The boogeyman, yes, and the Little Green Men from space, okay!

Ironically, the bogeyman appeared at night to Norman when we were in our room. It was associated with the light going off and on in the closet.

"Bev, there's a boo-gey-man in the closet," Norman said as he awoke me in the night. I tried to reassure him that there was no such thing; but he would not believe me. Orlando teased him so often, that he really believed there was one.

"It's just the light, Norman. There's something wrong with it," I pleaded. "Just go back to sleep."

"No Bev," Norman said as he sat straight up in the bed and stared mysteriously at the closet door. There was a trace of yellow light seeping through the doorway opening. With his eyes narrowing in the dark, he repeated slowly with a heaviness in his words, "There is someone in there. I'm sure."

I was never able to convince Norman that no one was in the closet; so, a number of times, I jumped out of bed, which really got on my 'last little nerves,' and walked into the closet. He followed, darting his head from side to side behind me. We never turned on the light, because this might wake our parents in the next room, and they would think something was wrong.

I stood on a small, wooden stool that we used to reach and turn on the light. The actual light fixture was not working. So, our father improvised by using an electrical brown cord attached to a brass pendant light socket with an on-off switch. He tied the brown cord into a knot nearest the bulb and hung it from a nail hammered into the wood molding. When I think back, this certainly was not a safe thing to do. But this was not my father's specialty. He should have asked Orlando to fix the light.

***

"Look Norman," I said as I picked up a soft rag I stuffed in the corner, so I would not burn my hand – which happened before, and turned the screw threads of the bulb, until it went off. "See, there is no boogeyman, Norman."

"Are you sure Beverley?" he asked, frightened still.

"Sure. "I TOLD YOU, there's no boogeyman!"

"I don't know, Bev. It seemed like one to me." Norman eyed the closet suspiciously; then ran out, jumped in the bed and covered his head with the blanket. I had four rubber pink-faced baby dolls with big eyes sitting on the closet floor near my toy kitchen set and bed furniture. Late at night their faces looked a little strange, particularly if the light struck their glass pupils in a certain way. I'm sure Norman was not comfortable with their eyes and this probably added to his fears.

I must admit I was scared of the Little Green Men in the fifties. There were talks of these little creatures on television and in the Indianapolis Star newspaper my parents subscribed to. This whole arena of UFO's and extraterrestrials dominated our media world. 'Look Magazine' for which my parents also had a subscription had articles about these creatures, and Orlando read these news clippings to us. Orlando also had comic books about these little men, which I looked at over and over.

Orlando told us they were small, skinny little men who could easily jump out the corner sewer/water drain systems. They came to America by way of flying saucers. I believed him and when Norman or I passed those drains in the evening, we walked far around them. The truth was, we jumped as far away from those openings as we could, day or night. The other neighborhood children did the same.

Like I said, I did not understand Norman's fear of his shadow. How did this happen? But in the summer evenings Orlando or sometimes our mother would take us to the corner Rexall Drug store for ice-cream cones or cherry cokes and French fries prepared at the fountain. The drinks had lots of ice, served in huge Styrofoam take home cups and the fries were taken from piping hot oil and quickly drained. On the corner across the street from the drug store stood a vintage cast-iron street lantern post, with a large frosted glass globe shining brightly over the intersection. This is where Norman's shadow would appear and scare the daylights out of him.

"He's gonna' get me!" he screamed. "He's gonna' swallow me up!" and Norman took off running.

Norman was right that his shadow was chasing him, because it was him, the dark area created when something blocked the light source that cast down on him.

I could not reason with him.

"Look, I have one too! See!" I pointed. Norman looked. "We all have one."

But somehow, Norman was persuaded his shadow was out to get him; and there was nothing I could do but run 'like the dickens' as fast as I could, with my skinny legs following his bowlegs.

The street lantern accentuated his shadow; and as he ran, his shadow ran right along with him, attached to his shoes. Norman was determined, however, to outpace the monster attached to his high-top tennis shoes, and that boy would run like there was no tomorrow.

By the time we got to the steps of our front porch, we were both sweating and musty, our chests heaving up and down, fast at first, then slower as we sat, and our breathing calmed. Sometimes, I could hear the leaves rustling in the large maple tree on our front lawn and caught the awakening sound of cicadas, while feeling the moisture slowly evaporate from my warm body. That felt really nice!

***

During the summer, Orlando went to the corner parking lot behind the drug store. This was the gathering place for teenage boys. My father never knew he hung out there with his friends, or he would not allow it. My father called them hooligan, even though some of the boys attended our church. "No home training," he ranted.

They were neighborhood boys, many of them older with nothing to do. Not like Orlando who had chores at the house: starting the family dinner, cutting the grass, trimming the hedges, weed, picking up the cutting piles left by our father, taking care of the fishpond, painting the trimming on the house, the fence lines in the backyard, and every two years, he and my mother painted every room in the house.

When Norman and I went to bed about midnight after watching a summer movie, that was when Orlando and our mother started painting. My father bought gallons of paints in the colors we selected. Our beds were moved to the center of the room. When we woke up, every room upstairs was painted.

The next night the twosome painted the living room, entry hall, and the lower half of the dining room. The upper part was wall papered, separated by a strip of wood molding. The kitchen and the breakfast nook were painted the following day.

Our father at first painted all the white wood trim in our house; but later, it became the job for Norman and me. Yes, Orlando had plenty to do.

Knowing our mother would send us back to get him, Orlando came home right away when we said, "Mother wants you." I guess he knew how painstaking another trip would be for

Norman, who was afraid of his shadow. Interestingly enough, Orlando never teased Norman about this fear.

As a young man, Norman faced a number of fears, some of his own doings, others an integral part of life we cannot escape, emotionally or figuratively. Our experiences prepare us for other aspects of life, certainly crucial to the persons we became. Ironically, it was not only my experiences which shaped and redirected my life, but my brothers' experiences as well.

Norman went on to enlist in the Navy, became a paramedic and later served as a detective with the police department from where he retired. He was confident in his ability to help others face their fears, possibly from being that little boy so distrustful of a world he didn't understand. Yet, he was willing to sacrifice his life for mankind in the military, serving time in Viet Nam. He was probably stronger than the rest of us having to reconcile our father's irritational racial ignorance in his own life, because of the color of his skin, while living the life of a Black man in America. He never seemed angry about his life. He embraced it.

9

Polio

We walked quietly from our first-grade classroom. The last student in line was the coat monitor whose responsibility was to make sure our belongings were properly locked up. As we walked down the hallowed halls, step by step, I felt a tingle of nervousness. Yet, I smiled at my classmates, putting on a brave face, that I did not feel, as we journeyed to our destination.

Leading our classroom was a nurse in a white pressed uniform, wearing a starched Florence Nightingale hat, talking to our teacher. We, however, were not allowed to talk. As the class approached the assembly hall, the noise level intensified. I could hear children crying. Every now and then, a child's scream, sent my heart racing through my body. We were going to be vaccinated for polio.

In a long line, waiting and watching, frightened kids were yelling and crying. Now I saw students pushing teachers and kicking nurses in their struggle to get away. This was definitely not a pleasant experience. We backed up as the ruckus continued in front of us. Teachers trying to take charge, yelling "Stop that young man!" and other things in the confusion. Sweat started to bead on my forehead, and I could feel the moisture under my short sleeve blouse (which we were asked to wear to expedite the procedure).

The noise in the assembly hall was overwhelming, with continuous student cries coming from everywhere, and loud instructions from adults. I looked around as my teachers directed us to a portable station where an awaiting nurse with an assistant was preparing our vaccine in a hypodermic needle. This was our shot. I was scared! My heart was beating rapidly in my chest.

This polio was another hidden fear for us children. How was it that this virus could just attack you, leaving you without the ability to walk and in some cases, breathe? Where was this thing hiding? How did it get in our bodies? I was frightened, looked around, but couldn't see anything that could do this to us.

When I got home, I couldn't wait to tell my mother about this horrible experience. Norman did too. She signed the papers giving the school authorization to do this. My mother said she would talk with our father when he got home. It turned out he had health insurance for our family. So, from then on, we received our polio shots from a nice, quiet doctor's office downtown. We did not have to go on the excursion with our classes. We were the only children present in the doctor's office. None of that yelling, screaming and crying! My father would not allow it. That sort of behavior was not acceptable. It embarrassed him.

In my elementary school, I don't recall seeing any children with polio, but when I participated with the state's music program in middle school, there were children with polio. In high school, I also saw students stricken. They rode the elevators along with the teachers to different floors. The elevator operator and the teachers had keys.

One of the girls was in my orchestra class over the years, she also attended music camp, so I sort of knew her well enough. I was always concerned that she looked worn out, like she was on her last leg. She could drop at any second! I see her walking with legs flailing as she rotated her hips, in iron leg braces. Later in high school, she had a boyfriend who carried her books. Her face seemed much softer then.

10

Fingers

I stood there locked in a singleness I had not known. My third-grade classmates hurried past me, running to recess. I did not move, just stared. Then I slowly walked under the overhang attached to a building where the restrooms were located, never moving my eyes from what I saw. I had a better view from here and I was out of the hustle of students chasing each other and laughing. 'How could this be?' I thought. Two girls, standing near the chain-linked fence aligning the neighborhood street, were talking to each other in a friendly way. It was clear they were sisters, from their close resemblance. A younger boy joined them, in quick excitement, then ran off. I later learned he was their brother, but his hands were normal. They were like my own, like all the kids in the school; but his sisters' hands were like twigs on branches in the spring. No leaves to camouflage them.

I could not rip my eyes from the sight. Their hands were like delicate little branches, long and thin, extending out on all sides: the little finger, the ring finger, the middle finger, and the index finger of their hands. There were multiple fingers, each very much alive, growing like shoots from their narrow, soft looking, light brown hands. Yet, the fingers were agile, efficient like my own, except so many.

It became an obsession of mine to just watch the girls from afar, fascinated by the appendages, animated and very much a part of their lives. I saw my brother talk to the younger boy on occasions: just things like greetings, "Hey man, (trying to talk like the big boys) how ya' doing? You gonna' play basketball with us on Friday?" things like that.

The sisters were however always together. I never saw one without the other or any other girls with them. I don't know if they had the same classes or if they had been placed together to support each other. They were definitely not the same age.

I had so much to learn in this new world in Indiana that our family moved to from Jamaica, BWI. There was so much to see, so many things that were different, unusual, but it didn't make them worse or horrible. I saw these two girls creating a new normal, a normal for them, certainly not one I understood. The girls were always neatly dressed, looked pleasant and it was clear they were well cared for with hair neatly combed, which is something Black girls have trouble with initially, until they mastered their own hair. Generally, we needed our mother, older sisters, grandmothers or aunts to comb our hair. Not like our brothers who could just run a brush through theirs.

I looked up multiple fingers in the encyclopedia. My father bought a set for our family, paying a monthly fee, that the salesman came to our home to collect. Polydactyly was the name applied to multiple fingers or toes. I never looked at their feet, because they wore enclosed tennis shoes like all the kids wore in spring. In the winter, we wore boots or galoshes. The book said, this condition is more common in men than women. Although when I saw the sisters, I assumed girls were most affected. The Encyclopedia Britannica also said this condition was more familiar among African Americans, although I've never seen it in any other friend or classmate of mine.

I know it was not nice to stare at the girls, but frankly, I found them fascinating; and to be quite honest, I was actually afraid. That's why I distanced myself from them. What if that happened to me or to my friends and family? So, I never got close to the girls, never even talked to them. The most we exchanged over the years was just a distant smile. I went on about my business and they went about theirs. It's funny how fear can separate classmates. It can channel us into avenues we would never have considered. My fears were exposed and my prejudices.

Yes, I was different too, but you could only tell when I spoke. I had a sight Jamaican accent, and so did my parents. Their accents were so strong that my friends came over and wanted to talk to my mother. They said they loved her accent. I never really heard it. I guess my mother's kind voice was already translated in my head, comforting! I recognized my father's accent all my life, wrapped around his meanness.

***

When I think back over the years, I hope that I didn't participate in making the girls lives more difficult, although I knew I had; because I never went over and talked to them. Never told them my name. But still I wanted the best for them, as I'm sure they wanted that for me. I was not a mean girl, and frankly, did not know many mean girls at that age. I was just too afraid to admit it. I was too afraid to get to know them.

***

One day, busy watching the sisters as usual, one of my classmates tapped me on the shoulder. Startled, I turned to face her. She placed her hands in front of my face. I looked at them and then gave her a puzzling look. What was she doing? Then she took her right hand and pointed. I saw a small nodule on the outside of her baby finger. She rotated her other hands so I could see there was also a nodule on the outside of her other hand.

I looked, wondering why she was showing me these little things, smaller than the top of a pencil eraser. Then she spoke, "I had an extra finger, on each side, which they removed when I was a baby. Then she giggled and said, "Come on," as she pulled me onto the playground to join the other children.

***

In 2003, I was reading about Bernini, a sculptor, in an article entitled, "Bernini and the Excesses of Art!" by Robert Peterson. Lian L. Bernini was a great baroque sculptor. He sculpted the Goddess Daphne, pursued by an aggressor, Apollo, the Greek God of music, poetry, art, and great warrior. Aberrant activities were going on everywhere in Rome. The goddess, knowing she had little chance to out-run Apollo, begged her father, Peneus, the river god, to help her. Her father answered her plea with a heavy numbness that transformed her body. Daphne stopped, then dramatically turned to stone, as her fingers became branches of the laurel tree. Apollo loved the laurel tree, and later gifts of the laurel tree were given as prizes. The sculpture embodied the loveliness of the goddess and her connection to nature with the tree.

I found it ironic that the goddess' name was Daphne, which is my mother's name. My mother ran from childhood poverty and escaped it as an adult.

When I saw the picture of Bernini's sculpture, I was immediately reminded of the sisters at my elementary school. That was how their hands looked. The comparison was uncanny, from a sculpture done in the 1800's, to schoolgirls in the 1950's.

How was this possible? Did Bernini in the 18th century see some beautiful lady with these hands? Were the sisters related to Daphne, long-lost cousins? Were these girls in the blood lineage of the goddess, extending back to Greek mythology? Rhetorical questions, yet to be answered, if ever.

***

In junior high school, I didn't see the sisters anymore, although their brother was still around. He played basketball with Norman and his buddies every now and then. I don't know if the girls went to live with grandparents or what; but they never appeared again in my life and I never saw anyone with such unique hands like theirs, ever, again.

II

Cruelty

I don't know where Orlando got the dog. Maybe, the dog just followed him home. My brother had such a kinship with animals. He could patch up injured birds and released them when they could fly. He and animals had a special affinity.

This night was one of those horrible Indiana winters, when the temperature was easily 10 to 15° below zero. Today, the weatherman or meteorologist (pick your choice) talks about Windchill factors. That information wasn't available when I was a child. But I know cold, yes, freezing cold.

We begged our father to let our new puppy come inside. He was so joyful and playful. The puppy was a breed with very short black hair, long thin legs and big clumsy paws. He was so happy when we played with him earlier; but our father said, "No! You think money grow on trees? Who will pay for him?"

Possibly, it was because we already had a family dog, Rex. He allowed Rex to be in the basement during the winter, and Rex would snuggle up near the big fat furnace to keep warm. Our father was angry that Orlando brought another dog home.

We begged our father to keep the dog in the basement that night. Orlando said he would take him to the pound the next day, but our father would not give in. I heard the dog crying as I tried to sleep that night. My heart ached for him, lonely, shivering in the cold, and the snow kept coming down.

The next morning, I jumped up and dressed when I heard my older brother stirring in the next room. Norman got up too. With coats on and snow boots, we followed Orlando outside. None of us spoke, as we anticipated what we would find.

We didn't have to go far before we saw the puppy, covered in a mound of snow, head and body buried, as his black legs stuck straight up through the untouched white snow, like a beast of burden in a barren field. The happy little puppy was hard as a rock, now a carcass. I looked at Orlando's face, red from the cold and anger building up within him, eyes icy. He pulled the puppy out of its ice incrusted grave and placed him respectfully into a plastic bag and took him to the alley. Norman and I watched, then looked sadly at each other. My heart fell to my stomach, reverberating like a timpani drum in my chest. My eyes were tearing, I'm sure for the dog, but I also had dry eye symptoms during the winter. With my mitten hands in my coat pocket, I didn't try to wipe my tears away. I blinked my glassy eyes as the sun was bright in the sky. I didn't know if I should also be mad at the sun.

When Orlando returned from the alley, we followed him inside. I was a cold, broken brown twig.

Norman said, "Why'd he looked like that?"

Orlando glanced at us. "Rigor mortis set in," he replied as he walked past, dismissing us. I guess he just wanted some time to himself.

'Rigor mortis,' I made a face. I didn't know what that was, but I knew cruelty.

How could our father do this? What kind of man would do this to a defenseless, loving animal? I was numb, frozen like our puppy with ice crystals on the fur of his black hind legs.

I hated my father.

12

Stain

Later, I must admit I am ashamed to tell you of my part. Norman asked me to help him lighten his skin. He wanted to be brown like me, not dark brown. I thought about it for a while. "Please Bev," he begged. "Help me. You can come up with something. I know you can."

So, when I was six and Norman was seven, I concocted a procedure that might bring him some hope. We sat on the mini striped carpet of the up-stairs hall. I took two bottles of shoe polish belonging to my father from the bathroom cabinet, a shiny black and dark brown.

Sitting on the carpet next to Norman, I pulled the applicators gently from the bottles, breaking the seal as the liquid started to bubble to the surface from displaced air. Each small glass bottle oozed with dark liquid at the top until the cotton lollipop-like applicator expelled from the bottle. Norman watched me intently. I placed the front page of the Indianapolis Star newspaper under his legs. Then I started painting stripes of black and brown shoe polish over Norman's lower legs, from beneath his knee to his ankle, and waited until the finish dried.

Norman, staring at the added colors, said nothing. He just sat comfortably in his safari shorts and high-top tennis shoes, which we folded down. I'm thinking, 'If he saw his skin had this beautiful shade of chocolate brown, he might like it, and our father and the mean world outside could not tear him up about it.'

As the polish dried, Norman's skin crinkled under the coating into weird wrinkle-like patterns. I got up from the floor, walked into the bathroom, and turned the hot water on as I pulled old rags out from under the sink. Norman didn't move, just waited for me; seemingly confident I could actually help him. Taking my role seriously, I carefully washed off the polish. I felt like a doctor removing blood from his legs.

"Did it work, Bev," my brother asked with excitement edging in his voice as his eyes brightened. He stared into my eyes again.

"Sure did, it worked just fine." There was such a contrast between the dark colors of the polish and my brother's skin, that surely Norman could see he wasn't a 'black' boy.

"Thanks Bev," he said with a smile gently crossing his face, as he straightened his shoulders with confidence. His cotton striped shirt and khaki Bermuda shorts came to attention as he moved.

We got up from the floor. I took the soiled rags, hardened now, out to the trash bin in the alley. Norman and I never talked about the incident ever again. I guess we never talked about it, because it worked. It worked in the minds of children.

***

We were just trying to make sense of a world where black boys were not valued, and some police would gladly take them down. I thought at the time that if I could show my brother that he wasn't black like my Sunday black patent leather shoes, I could help.

***

I saw racism, so alive in white America, creep its ugly head into my family, because it was taught to our father through propaganda from his time living in Panama, Great Britain and America. He believed, as learned, black men in the United States were lazy. My father never saw himself as a Black man in America. Anyone darker than himself was not worthy of his time and or his investment.

Regrettably, our father continued to act on his own prejudices. It was his ignorance that infested our home like pests, but my brothers and I were not able to escape its vapors of fumigation. My mother was however impenetrable. She knew well the cruelty of exclusion, and she was not dark, from her rough childhood with her mean aunt who hated her and treated her, this little girl, like she was beneath them, because she was abandoned by her mother. Her mother was sent to live in Cuba with relatives after an unwanted pregnancy. Her father was told by my maternal great-grandfather, never to come to their home again, or "Me will kill you." And so, my mother was beneath her! That is what her aunt believed.

My father refused to pay Norman's book rental fees and lunch money, because he said Norman was too dark to be his son. My mother took money from our father's wallet as he slept to pay for Norman school needs. Norman wanted me to change his skin color, because of my father's racism. I tried to do this by camouflaging his skin with shoe polish stain. I didn't know then that this was never possible, only in the mind of a child.

We grew up in the Jim Crow era of "Act your age, not your color," commonly said and definitely practiced.

Norman on his own developed the confidence needed, because he was popular among his friends, girls sought after him, and handsome as a child and a man. Norman was the only child of our father, Reverend Norman Matthews, who was the split image of our grandfather, our father's father. My father didn't like his father, because he believed it was his fault that their family went from 'well to do' to ruin.

13

Horror Film

Standing at the footboard of my mother's mahogany bed, I waited. I was excited, still in my nightgown. I watched my mother's reaction as she telephoned the radio station that was giving away free tickets to the headliner Frankenstein movie. It was 6:20 in the morning, and she waited on the phone for seemingly fifteen minutes until an operator took her call.

My mother was ecstatic. All she had to do was scream the loudest on the telephone, and she would win a set of tickets to the movie theater, enough for her, my brothers and me. Anticipating her performance, I was so nervous. I hadn't heard her scream before. I saw her run really fast one day, because she was afraid of a caterpillar crawling up the back of my dress. Orlando removed it. I knew her vigorous laughter, because my friends liked to come over and talk and laugh with her. She could scream, I'm sure. I knew she could. Eerie however, I also understood if she won, my brothers and I would be headed to the show to watch that scary film with her. She would never go alone, because that was not something women would do in those times; and my father thought films were foolishness, and he would never attend.

"It's simply a complete waste of time and money, D," my father said to my mother. He called her 'D' when he was in a decent mood, short for Daphne. "You think you American, eh?" My father shrugged his head and shoulders back, indicating my mother just didn't get it.

My mother laughed. "Just watch me," she said quite smugly. She didn't debate with my father about whether she was American or not. She got what she wanted, and that was definitely American to me.

Movies were her favorite pastime, and her passion was the horror genre. So, it didn't matter to her what my father said.

In fact, that particular morning, my father was not home. He left for a 5:30 a.m. job at the Mechanic's Laundry. Sometimes, Norman's friends would tease us about all the jobs our father had. 'American man, one job! Jamaican man, three jobs, mon!' They laughed, and we did too.

My mother held the black acrylic phone handset and waited. She turned to look at me periodically with a big smile. I returned her smile. I could see sweat banding on her forehead, but she looked confident.

Norman walked sleepily into the room. Orlando was already sitting in the padded tweed swivel armchair on top of clean clothes my mother had washed and folded the night before. His right leg raised and spread across the thick arm of the rocker, with his left foot touching the floor.

This was my mother's performance day, and she was ready as if she was going to recite lines from Elizabeth Barrett

Browning's Sonnet, "How do I love thee? Let me count the ways…."

They must have finally given her clearance, because she said assuredly, "I'm ready." I could feel a little stirring in my stomach and tension mounting in my chest and neck.

I took a deep breath as I watched my mother take one too. She paused. I waited, and then she let out this ungodly scream that could have been heard from one corner of our neighborhood to the next. I felt like I had been knocked to the floor from the sheer volume and intensity of her scream, as I cradled my head in my arms with my fingers covering my ears. I was really frightened even though I knew her scream was fake; but it scared the living daylights out of me.

My brothers were yelling with laughter and I started laughing to, feeling so stupid for actually being frightened. My mother stopped screaming. She was waiting. Shortly, the operator told her she was in the top five. With her hand covering the mouthpiece, she turned and relayed this information to us. They would know shortly who the winner was.

We all waited.

Anxiously, Norman finally uttered, "Did she win?"

Orlando and I quickly shushed him. His eyes brightened and stood out like almonds in his head, his face with a puzzling look like, 'what's going on here?'

The waiting continued. Tiny beads of sweat were more pronounced on my mother's forehead, and I watched as they flattened and slowly trickled down her face, even though it was chilly outside, a typical October morning.

It seemed like a lifetime before our mother yelled, "I won!" The pandemonium and celebration were so much fun. We were jumping up and down, yelling and screaming, diving on to my mother's bed. Hugging each other. She did it! We were happy! Free tickets and my mother said we would get complimentary popcorn and drinks too. What a day! We left my mother's bedroom to get ready for school. My mother dropped us off and then she went to work.

Two weeks later, the tickets arrived in the mail along with our passes for popcorn and drinks. We were so excited, particularly our mother. She was 'all smiles' and nothing could 'rain on her parade.' We were going to the movies and did not have to pay anything. It was FREE! I don't know even one of my friends' mothers who would have done this screaming match competition. My mother was pretty special!

A Saturday afternoon matinee was planned for our outing. It was cold outside, so we wore our school khaki car-coats, hats and gloves. Norman and I had similar jackets, except mine was pink, and his was army green. We took the bus, and as always, the bus was full; but it didn't matter to us, because this was going to be a fun day. My father said he would pick us up when we were ready. I was surprised by his willingness to do this. Just what was he up to, I wondered. He never offered to take us anywhere; but maybe he thought he might get something out of the experience our mother had screamed the loudest for; and ironically, he did not have to work that Saturday.

We saw the marquee announcing the movie "Frankenstein" as we walked up to a ticket booth, about 4' x 6', paneled with white bulbs and red neon lights outlining its rectangular shape. My mother showed the young lady our tickets and she directed us to the entrance of the theatre where a man was standing in the doorframe. He was wearing a small, round box hat in two colors, red and navy, with gold piping circling the circumference of the hat. He was a neatly shaven older white man. In addition to the hat, a matching navy colored cropped jacket was practically plastered to his chest, with at least four rows of buttons, (two rows on each side). He looked very much like he belonged in the military, with equivalent creased trousers.

When the usher swung the curtains back, I looked into the theatre. It was dark at first, but as my eyes adjusted, I saw the majestic burgundy velvet drapes with gold tasseled rope trim hanging from the top. 'Wow,' I thought. I had not been in a theatre this large, nor this luxurious. All the chairs were upholstered in the velvet burgundy as well. I ran my fingers across the velvet, which was interesting to the touch. Little fiber stood straight up, like rubbing the head of a Labrador Retriever.

Before the film began, my mother took us to the refreshment stand. Aside from our freebies, she also allowed us to buy candy, and we all shared one order of chips with cheese. When we returned to our seats, it was dark. We settled in. I rested my car coat on the back of my seat. I sat next to mother, then Norman and Orlando. The presentation started with Looney Tune cartoons. We really laughed. It was going to be a fun day. However, when the feature started, the accompanying music, and darkness made me quite uncomfortable. In anticipation, I pulled my coat from the back of my chair to my front. I placed my hands inside so I could use my coat as a coverup when needed.

When Frankenstein slowly began coming to life, moving initially his fingers, I inched my coat towards my face. The fear in me took control, as I heard my mother screaming and laughing. I was so frightened, I excused myself to go to the restroom. Norman came with me. My mother and Orlando were really enjoying themselves. Luckily, we were seated on the back row of the orchestra section, so we did not disturb the people behind us in the middle section. I tried to stay in the restroom as long as I could, not wanting Norman to think I was sick, nor I did not want him to know how scared I was.

When I returned to my seat, I covered my face completely with my coat; but the movie soundtrack was just as compelling and frightening. I could not wait to get out of there. My mother was, however, quite happy.

14

Hold on Kids

After we were out of city limits, where there were no stop signs or signal lights, my mother shouted, "Hold on kids," as she pressed 'the pedal to the metal' with her left elbow on the driver's window frame, looking cool, we agreed. We grabbed the base of our seats and braced our backs as the centrifugal force plastered our bodies to the car against the vinyl cushions and to each other.

Our hearts pounded in our chests and we laughed as the exhilaration took us into an oblivion I could not imagine, other than maybe a roller coaster.

Having grown up in the city, the cornfields of Indiana were truly amazing. I never saw so much land. It was like traveling in another world. My mother was happy too. She had a new car, a white Chrysler Plymouth, which my father bought so she would not have to wait for him to pick her up from work. When our family went out, no one wanted to ride with my father who only wanted to discuss religious parables, and he hated the music we listened to anyway. He said our music was sheer foolishness and decadent. So, most of the time he drove alone, and us children piled into our mother's car like sardines. We could hear our tunes on the radio and my mother sang along with us.

In the summer, one of my mother's activities after church was to drive through the cornfields, like she was navigating the Indianapolis 500, or commonly said "like a bat out of hell," but we were not allowed to say that.

Jim Crow laws dictated what we, Black people in Indianapolis, could or could not do. So, my mother created an amusement of her own making.

So many people, both Black and white, were employed by the automobile industry, GM, Ford and Chrysler, in Indiana that no one cared about a Black family with a new car. It was seen as contributing to the economy when you drove an American car. Cars were the rage in Indiana.

Traveling back-and-forth from the designer log cabin belonging to the grandparents of the people my mother worked for and to the Colonial mansion where my mother worked, she learned many secluded routes. Some routes were filled with thick cornhusks almost as tall as our car, and others were even taller hiding the carload of us from the road as shiny leafy maize smacked the side of my mother's vehicle as she sped through the dirt roads.

Our vehicle was blanketed in brown dust as I blinked my eyes to keep from tearing. With all four windows down creating a firestorm of fury with the humidity, the wind slapped our faces, created a drone sound in our ears, and the sun baked our already brown arms and bodies; but we were excited.

***

On those Sundays, when my mother's voice howled, "Hold on Kids!" through the unrelenting breeze racing through the car, it became our time to ride, fast and high into the dirt filled air. No Jim Crow laws! We were on private property with permission to be there. Her words were accompanied by an intense wind that initially bellowed past us, then through us as we became malleable, and finally into us, reaffirming our bond with our mother, the malevolent forces we had yet to encounter, and to each other.

***

"Hold on Kids" became for me a metaphor for my life, instilled by our mother! She was gentle, yet firm, humorous, yet appropriately compassionate, witty as she learned this new world of America. Jamaica, her birthplace, was long gone. Her words still echo through my mind, bringing me back to those special times, carefree, yet holding on to the framework our mother created.

***

Just before the gravel path became asphalt again and a red flashing stop light miraculously appeared, my mother returned to her law-abiding self, very sophisticated. We, her children, exhaled, smiling, looking around and at each other, as well as looking for cops. We learned a lot on those excursions.

15

Green Apples

Eddie was about eight years old. I watched him from two rows behind as he sat with his buddies on the front pew of the church. He looked really nice in his little dark suit as he turned around and nervously smiled at me, then quickly turned back. Eddie was one of the pallbearers that day for his friend Paul. All the boys looked like little men in their Sunday suits in memory of their playmate who died from appendicitis.

Eddie and his chums were doing what all kids did in Indiana in the springtime, eating green apples. We just couldn't wait for them to ripen on the tree, so we ate them green. When you first bit into the un-ripened fruit, the taste was really tart and your face would pucker, as your eyes blinked, and your neck tightened. The texture was really hard. You took small bites until all the apple was gone, then of course, you ate several more.

Not only did we eat apples that were not ripe, we also ate red and green grapes, peaches, mulberries, pears (they were like rocks) and cherries, fruits from our neighbors' yards. Generally, we asked permission if it was not the home of one of our friends. We just could not wait.

From what I heard, when the boys got home, Paul complained to his mom about a stomachache. She chastised him for eating all those green apples, then assured him it would pass. The next morning when she went to wake her son, he was semi-conscious, and she rushed him to the hospital. It was there she learned that his appendix had burst sending bacteria into his system. The doctor said if he'd come in a day earlier, he may have survived, but unfortunately for the family, it was too late.

I kept an eye on my younger brother wondering how he would manage with his friend's death. The quick nervous smile he gave me earlier was not a good indicator of how he was really feeling. I believe it was his innocent way of reassuring me he was alright, and that I should not worry about him. But I am his older sister, and did not want him in sorrow, although I knew I could not change life.

I felt so terrible for his friend's mother. Paul was her only child, and certainly for Eddie and his buddies. This was such an early age to face life challenges.

After Paul's death, my brother and his buddies connected most days with each other, playing kickball, racing to "On Your Mark, Get set, Ready, Go!" while laughing, and joking as life went on. It pained me to see his friend was missing. After that, we seldom saw the boys trying to get apples from the apple trees or any of the fruit trees; but my brother still enjoyed eating the baked apple pies I made for the family from our tree.

16

Fitzpatrick

Nearing exhaustion, Norman and I ran from the center of the regulation tennis court, put our rackets on the green turf, and bent over, panting. With our hands on our knees, Norman's smooth chocolate skin looked like it had been polished in the sunlight. We took penetrating breaths. I felt the air going through my lungs. I looked around, heard the chirping of birds in the tall acorn trees, smelled a faint scent of a nearby sassafras which immediately reminded me of early morning hikes at Girl Scout Camp. I examined the leaf of the sassafras and tasted its stringent stem, used for teas. That sense of smell has always stayed with me. Nearby, the small green leaves of elm trees rustled quietly in the wind, with squirrels chasing each other through the maze of their branches.

The sky was baby blue, crystal clear, not a trace of a cloud, just this calming presence, typical of a summer morning. I loved this feeling, this time of day. I was caressed by nature.

Norman stood. I hadn't noticed. He took another breath and said happily as he chuckled, "I beat you Bev. You can't keep up with the big boys."

"You did not," I said a little too hastily, "Well, just maybe a bit," I softened and smiled. Now we were both standing straight as our breathing returned to normal. Eddie was running with his little legs barely leaving the turf across the tennis court, picking up balls, giggling as he threw balls towards us.

"Watch it little man," Norman said smiling, then, he threw a tennis ball back at Eddie.

***

It was hard to believe we were playing tennis on a tennis court. In Indianapolis, courts were not opened to Negroes. Because we were on private property where my mother worked as a housekeeper/nanny, we could play, not really knowing the rules. Although Norman seemed to understand the rules of scores, "Love, Ad in, etc."

***

Eddie was getting ready to throw another ball, when we heard our mother shout from the mansion door, "Hey kids, get the rackets and tennis balls and come in. We will be having visitors soon."

Visitors, I wondered who it could be. Earlier, Orlando left with Henry, one of the workers, to help at the farm. The family my mother worked for was in Europe for the summer. Every couple of years, the doctor would buy a new Mercedes Benz in Germany, and have it shipped back to the United States, which I thought was really classy.

108

Periodically, Norman and I went to the garage to look at the Mercedes left behind, admiring its burgundy leather interior and seats, Burl wood dashboard, a chrome plated cigarette lighter and ashtray, clock, odometer, padded leather steering wheel, column and accessories.

So now, who else knew we were here?

When we got to the enormous front door, my mother stood in its massive frame. "The doctor's brother and his son are coming this afternoon. They flew in this morning on his private plane from Florida. I want you kids to meet them."

My mind started revving up. 'Is this the son who flies the family plane, and he is our age,' I thought?

"You remember Fitzpatrick? I've told you about him. Quite a remarkable boy," my mother said proudly.

"Yes, I remember," I said and flashed Norman an inquisitive look.

Norman looked up and I saw his eyebrows, really nice ones, not thin like mine. They were arched high on his brow, like they were trimmed by a makeup artist. He also had nice curly hair, not thin like my own.

"You kids put the rackets away and get cleaned up," my mother continued. "They should be here by noon. They are at the grandparent's log cabin now."

I envisioned the log cabin in my mind. This was not the typical cabin you saw on TV. This one had colossal logs, shiny from coats of some kind of finish, like polyurethane on the outside. The massive home was one you could imagine in a fairytale. Beautiful! Definitely, designer!

***

"Neat-O," Eddie shouted!

Not sure why Eddie was so excited, but little kids liked having company, because they might get something special, like candy.

Norman and I started walking towards the large laundry room with its hefty washer and dryer. The lower cabinets were loaded with Borax soap, Ivory bars in wax paper, Tide detergent, Clorox bleach, apple cider vinegar, Scott's toilet paper - individually wrapped in tissue paper they purchased by the case, Pine Sol, all kinds of cleaning products, etc. There was a counter for folding clothes, an iron with a padded ironing board, and a deep soaking utility sink. That is where we washed up. We got soft washcloths from the Butler's Pantry, the room across from the laundry room.

I thought the Butler's Pantry was so nice, neatly organized. The cabinets were painted white, with French windows across the upper cabinets where plates, cups and saucers, and crystals used for parties for more than a hundred people were stored. Silverware probably silver plated, certainly not sterling, my mother cleaned, was kept in the top drawer beneath the counter. Coffee urns and teapots were stored in the lower cabinets of the pantry. The large drawer next to the door held the white fluffy washcloths, which my mother washed and returned to that compartment.

***

I was a little nervous about meeting Fitzpatrick, after all, he didn't sound like a kid to me, more like a miniature man.

When the gong of the antique Grandfather clock sounded, the face of the moon and sun shyly rotated across its glass surface. Bongs rang out as the front doorbell rang simultaneously. My mother, who never wore a uniform – just regular house clothes, walked to the door and answered it and I heard a man's voice say, "Well, hello Daphne!"

"Kids," my mother turned and hollered, "They're here!"

We walked from the large black and white checkered porcelain tile floors in the laundry room and hallway, onto the adjacent entry hall.

In the majestic entry hall, Fitzpatrick stood next to his father, erect, as he had been taught in military boarding school, no doubt. I could imagine him standing with his cadets at early morning reveille, not even blinking, as the sergeant walked past during inspection and formations. He smiled and nodded his head. His father said proudly they had just flown in from Florida. "My son here," as he slapped his shoulder, "did all the flying."

Fitzpatrick had a big smile now on his face, as my mother raved over his accomplishment. I wanted to ask him, 'Were you afraid,' but I didn't? I was really impressed with this strikingly handsome young man, although he was really just a kid like me, but his experiences surpassed any we had or would ever have. Our family, in comparison, would be considered among the "Have Nots."

When he tipped his black, English riding helmet, a mop of straight blond locks fell effortlessly from the top of his head, hitting his eyebrows below. He shook his head to the side quickly and his hair went back in place. He was dressed in full gear riding apparel. He must have changed clothing at his grandparents' home. From the neck down, he wore a white cotton ascot, a worsted wool red cutaway riding jacket with a black velvet collar and tails, a forest green buttoned front vest, black French Jodhpurs riding breeches, shiny black leather boots that came up to his knees, and silver spurs at his ankles.

Fitzpatrick was quite stunning. He looked like he just stepped out of a Vogue magazine ad, with his sharp angular features, powdered blue eyes, long lashes, and skin like fine bone china, the ones you can see your hand through. It was hard for me not to stare at him, which was considered rude; but he was the most gorgeous person I'd seen, and he was a boy. He was strikingly exquisite. I wanted to enjoy his beauty, but shifted my eyes from time to time, not wanting to appear ill-mannered.

The doctor's brother told my mother Fitzpatrick was riding in a tournament that afternoon, and they needed to borrow a riding crop belonging to his brother's son, his nephew. Fitzpatrick ran effortlessly up the steps, light on his feet and was back down with the riding crop in a flash. I wondered if he noticed the Horn Toad Lizard in the glass case on his cousin's dresser.

I had to look closely to spot the lizard among the dried grasses, sticks, sand and rocks with its ability to camouflage itself. The lizard looked strangely prehistoric to me, like a miniature dinosaur with raised scaled horns on its back and head, and desert dry skin. His cousin left a cardboard box of live insects for Orlando to feed his toad each week while he was away, and my mother placed lettuce in his cage daily.

My mother offered to make them lunch, but Fitzpatrick's father said that with the tournament, it was better for his son not to ride with a full stomach, and they needed to get to the competition for Fitzpatrick to warm up.

Norman and I watched and smiled as they left, standing straight and tall as Fitzpatrick had done earlier. My mother walked them to their car door, as she continued talking with his father. Orlando and Henry drove up at the same time, and I was surprised to see Fitzpatrick get out of the car and hurry over to Orlando. They laughed and talked. It appeared Orlando had met him before, actually knew him. They seemed like buddies. Orlando, five years older than Norman and six years older than me, had that natural knack in meeting and greeting people, always making an impression. People never forgot him.

Norman and I stood back and watched the group from the massive front door, which swallowed us up in the frame. Fitzpatrick was far more animated now, as Orlando grabbed him across the shoulders and wished him well on his tournament later. Orlando walked back to the car with Fitzpatrick at his side and greeted his father who was seated at the steering wheel with the window down. His father spoke to Orlando, smiling. I could not hear what they were saying; but the look on my mother's face said it all. She was proud!

I thought Fitzpatrick was a pretty neat person, taking full advantage of what life had to offer. He was so comfortable getting out of the car and running up to Orlando, a Black person, and putting his arms around him. I thought maybe the fact he lived in Florida, affected how he saw and perceived Negroes, and he didn't need a Jim Crow sign displaying, "Whites Only," to tell him who to associate with.

When Fitzpatrick and his father drove off, Norman spoke for the first time, lowering his head; but his eyebrows and eyes were raised. "He's a pretty boy," Norman said quietly, so our mother would not hear, and nonchalantly like he had heard this phrase many times said. "That's what they call them at school."

But Fitzpatrick wasn't just pretty, he was gorgeous! He must have gotten his looks from his mother, because his father was plain looking like the rest of us.

***

Twenty years later, Norman and I ran into Fitzpatrick after his grandfather's death at the repast reception held at the magnificent log cabin house, which still looked the way I remembered, enchanting! That beautiful, angelic, blond hair Fitzgerald had was gone. But he still had those dazzling powder blue eyes, his endearing smile and personality. He greeted us like long lost relatives.

17

Music Room

I walked down the steep cement steps of the music room. This room certainly did not look like any classroom I had had. The cement floors were not covered with linoleum tiles or hardwoods that were in other parts of the school. The room was cavernous, with large storage lockers on one side of the room, and metal shades and bright bulbs extended from the ceiling on long poles. In the front was an office for the teacher with a phone and lots of shelves on the wall for printed music. I believe this area was originally storage for the custodial staff.

We were in the fourth grade when one of my classmates who played violin, told me the teacher was looking for a student to play the piano for the orchestra. I was confident I could do that, so I had gone along with her to the music room early one morning to meet the teacher and audition to see if I could play the piano parts. My class before lunch was changed so I could play with the orchestra.

Every day I went to class and for the most part, I just sat there, because there were few piano parts to accompany the orchestra. One day, the teacher said to me.
"Beverley, how would you like to play the viola?"

I did not really know what a viola was as I looked into his eyes. He immediately sensed my lack of knowledge, and told me about the instrument, larger and deeper in tone than the violin, but played the same way. However, it played a different clef, not the clef the piano played. I thought it would be a good idea, because I was getting bored waiting for my piano music to be required, and I 'm sure the teacher recognized this as well.

So, I started playing the viola and got pretty good at it over time. Later in high school, I was able to compete on the city and state levels in competitions. My teacher, even though his specialty was wind instruments, taught me the rudiments of playing the viola. Students paid a rental fee to play the instruments, but we could take the instruments home on weekends and vacations.

Later, my father bought me my own viola and agreed to pay for private lessons from a young white lady who played with the Indianapolis Symphony. My music teacher, who was Black, recommended her. She was very nice, and the lessons took place at her home. My mother would drop me off or wait for me, depending on her schedule. It was a one-hour lesson. I was winded by the time I got to her front door, because I had to carry my large viola up a number of steep steps.

***

One nice thing about having a little boyfriend in junior high was that he carried my instrument; otherwise, Norman would come by my class after school and carry my viola for me. I was small and thin, so I needed help.

My music teacher was such a nice man, but I sensed something different and troubling about him, lingering just under the surface. Sometimes, when I walked into his office, I could hear him arguing with someone on the phone, and I just assumed it was his wife. She came to our music room on a couple of occasions and I sensed she was angry with him.

Sometimes, we smelled alcohol on him. Once, my friend and I confronted him about it. He assured us he was not drinking, and that what we smelled was his cough medicine, which he took each morning for allergies. I didn't believe him; but continued to work with him. I thought it was important to tell him what we students thought, because maybe there was something, he could do to make corrections. He came to work every day and helped us with our instructions, which included the tune-up period at the beginning of every practice. This is when the alcohol odor was particularly strong.

When I learned to tune my own instrument, we no longer had this close proximity. Whether or not the smell was still there, became a mute-point, because he functioned well as a teacher with the orchestra class.

***

When I was in high school, I learned tragic news about him. Our music teacher committed suicide with a single bullet to the head. My mother shared the information from the newspaper with me. I was so sorry he was not able to get the help he needed. Certainly, the principal, assistant principal, teachers and the nurse should have known, especially when I as a fourth grader and my classmates knew. I was sorry. Addiction is a terrible illness.

***

The music room was not near any other classrooms. Large restrooms with multiple stalls were across the hall, and the primary classrooms were down the cement hall on the opposite end.

I remember walking down the long corridor as a first grader, proudly carrying our classroom fishbowl for cleaning in the restroom. It was a little awkward, trying not to spill the water, while caring for the fish. It was my job that week to clean the fishbowl. I loved the little goldfish, who splashed around and came to the surface when we fed them food, with mouths wide open.

During the cleaning, I was trying to be so careful, when one of the fish jumped out of the bowl. I tried to save him, but I could not. He was faster, and I was standing there with a glass bowl in one hand pressed against my chest, while using my other hand to clean the walls of the bowl with a small bristle brush. The fish was gone in the blink of an eye as I watched him slide down the drain. The other fish did not seem bothered by his escape. I was, however, crushed. When I returned to my classroom, nervous and anxious for what happened in the restroom, the teacher did not notice one of the fish was missing, or if she did, she didn't say anything, nor did I. My teacher was busy with all the usual things that happened every day at school.

***

My teacher was so talented. He could play all the instruments in the music room. He introduced me to the viola, started me on this road, and opened doors for me by doing so. He believed in his students and made sure we were well prepared. He had so much to offer; but like that fish from the glass bowl, he found a way to escape.

18

The Challenge

In the fifth grade, my mother asked me to sit down with her for a serious discussion. I wondered what this could be, after all, she only had me in the room as a quiet listener and observer. The discussion was not really a discussion at all. As she talked, I listened. The topic was strange to me and frightening. She wanted me to know what to do in the event of her death.

My heart dropped and I felt like my breathing stopped. I took a deep breath and as my chest filled with air, looked at my mother. Her eyes were like looking into a fishbowl, deep and penetrating. With her dark brown eyes swimming in tears, I couldn't understand why we were having this conversation. I wondered if our family doctor had said something about her health that she wanted me to know. Regardless, it was clear to me that my mother really believe she was not going to live to see her children grow up.

I knew that it was her depression talking, that's what our family doctor said she had. She told me that after a lifetime of hearing 'nothing good would come of her life,' having been told this over and over by her hateful aunt and her selfish mother, my mother now believed them. "Girl children nothing but trouble!... YOU NOTHING! Just a Bastard Child...." These comments from the two crucial women in her life marked her for doom and her confidence was too fragile to see beyond their predictions.

I listened to my mother not really believing that she would die soon, but recognized how important it was to her that I understood her position and would be there to take over the house and younger children in the event of her untimely death. Why wasn't my mother having this conversation with my father? Why was I the source of my mother's confidence? I was only 10 years old.

A good dinner cook I was not, never really having the practice. That was Orlando's job, and he was good at it, but I could do breakfast. I admit I deliberately burned my father's eggs, making them extra crispy in hot bacon fat so I would not have to prepare his breakfast anymore. I watch discreetly from the kitchen as my father tried to cut his eggs with his utensils, smiling to myself. I didn't burn the bacon, because I needed the oil to fry them. My father complained to my mother about his eggs. Norman was assigned the task of preparing our father's breakfast, when my mother left early for work.

But I could clean the house. I vacuumed every day. I loved it! My mother said later that when I left for college our home was never as clean. Every Saturday morning, our father woke Orlando, Norman, and me at 7 am. We got dressed, went downstairs, and ate a bowl of cereal. Then we got buckets and rags to start cleaning the woodwork in the entire house, all of which was painted white. Now there were six children, the three older ones and three younger ones. My father did not want to see any fingerprints on the baseboard or molding throughout the house and that included closet doors and cabinetry. I hated to put my hands in all that dirty water, having to empty the bucket and add fresh hot water to finish the job. I could not carry a lot, so my bucket was always half full.

My relationship with my father became more and more strained as my teenage years approached. When he would not listen to my reason, I shouted at him, "I hate you! I hate you!" and would run up the steps with my heart beating in my stomach to the bedroom I shared with my little sisters and slam the door. I stayed there until my mother got home. By that time, my father looked so crushed and emotionally wrecked, that my mother came to my room. She listened to what I had to say, then, insisted I go downstairs and apologized to my father who looked like little orphan Annie seated in his favorite chair. "There, little girl! Don't cry! They have broken your heart. I know, and the rainbow gleams of your youthful dreams...." *Life Lessons* by James Whitcomb Riley an Indiana poet. We read many of his works in school. I knew that I had to apologize to keep the peace in the family.

While my father could be bitingly cruel to his sons, rarely were those comments directed to me. However, on one occasion, my father was talking to me, but I did not know it. I would never be deliberately rude to my parents. My father knew I had little fear of him, even though I weighed less than

100 pounds. He probably thought I was off in my head. I was talking on the telephone that day, my back to him, when he walked up behind me. He used his massive hand, the one he wanted to train to be a fighter and struck me with a powerful blow to the side of my head. My ears rang and I saw flashes of reds, yellows, and black lights in geometric shapes with jagged edges as I fell to the floor. I was in a comic strip when the character hits the other one over the head with a club. I don't remember passing out, but I must have because everything was black and my left ear was burning and throbbing, the side of my face pulsating and my skin was reddened.

Norman came over to me as I lay on the dining room floor, leaned his face just above my own as my father abruptly rushed past. I was rubbish. I had wronged him and certainly not the other way around. I could feel Norman's warm breath hitting the surface of my clammy skin as he spoke quietly. "I'll help you Bev. You can tell mother, when she gets home." Norman helped me into a dining chair. I was dizzy and winded. My father was satisfied that when he speaks, you better listen! I stared at him with vindictive wrath with hot tears running down my icy cheeks.

My father continued, "If you can't hear, you'll feel!"

"Just wait until my mother gets home," I said in a chilling voice. I could see a muscle twitch in my father's thick neck as he turned to look at me.

"Don't say anything else Bev," Norman whispered as he laid his hand on my shoulder. "Mother will be here soon. I already called her."

I refused to allow my father's words to go unchallenged. Our father thought he was so brilliant. It was rare that my father said anything to me. I think because I was an A/B student. Orlando and Norman were C/D students, so he took pleasure in degrading them. I felt our father was the reason that they were poor students. They did not want to be like him. My father never bothered my younger brother Eddie, because he was an A student.

Norman was such a sweet child, neatly dressed; but he always begged me not to say anything back to our father. I could not appease him, watching our father take pleasure at our expense. If Orlando had been there, he would've been ready to fight, sporting hatred with furrowed eyebrows, white knuckles, and neck muscles pulsating. I could imagine his hands squeezed tightly next to his well-developed upper thighs, ready to defend me; but he knew if he did anything physical with our father, he would have to leave our home. Our mother made it clear, there could only be one man in the house. Norman was gentle and didn't say anything. He just stood there and took our fathers insults, looking seemingly blank like the words never crossed into his consciousness, which made my father even angrier.

***

When my mother arrived, she placed her warm, rough hands under my chin, and examined my face. She went directly upstairs to their bedroom, not saying anything. I could hear my parents yelling. Then my mother shouted, "If you ever touch that child again, I WILL KILL YOU!"

Norman said with a smile, "He won't bother you again, Beverley."

I was gratified my father was put in his place. It felt really good! I didn't care if he never spoke to me again. I just wanted him to stay away from me. My father never struck me again, and when passing me, he lowered his head, so I did not have to look at his mean hazel eyes. I kept my head and chest up.

***

That day, I believed my ten-year-old self had convinced my mother that I could be an adequate replacement to take care of the children and household, if she should unexpectedly die. I was good and patient with my younger siblings, giving them a bath every day, playing games with them, and teaching them parts to learn in our drama productions. If they didn't behave, I folded a newspaper, and gave them a couple of swats on their behinds. I ironed the clothes and kept the house clean. I could do it, you know, 'Be in charge,' if I had to. Like other children, I imagined my mother passed out at the car steering wheel, where I would gently push my mother into the passenger seat, (don't know how I would have done that with my 85 pounds) occupy the driver's seat, then drive her carefully to a hospital emergency center. But never did I think of my mother as dead! The challenge for me was my father. Without our mother as a formidable back up, he would make our lives miserable. There would be no one to keep him in check, and he would thrive on the cruelty he knew so well.

19

The Joke

I took my mother's special little gift to school. I don't remember if she gave me permission to take it. I was in the fifth grade and wanted to show my friends and classmates how unique this gift was. The gift was wrapped in a pretty package with all the trimmings of a wonderful surprise, including a bow on top; but it had a mechanical feature that when activated, a slinky clown jumped out of the cylindrical box.

During the passing period, a number of students surrounded me at my desk. The word spread quickly about my gift, and they wanted to see. When my teacher walked in, she directed the students to take their seats. I quickly stuffed the gift into the bag. I initially thought she didn't notice my package, until she said, "Beverley, bring that package to my desk." Now I was really nervous as my heart raced in my chest. What was she going to do with my gift? I picked up the bag with the gift inside and walked slowly to her desk.

"Is there something in there that you want to show me?" she asked.

"No Mrs. Blanton," I replied with a sick feeling in my stomach. My classmates were staring at me and I heard a few of them snicker.

Our teacher's desk was located in the back of the classroom.

She repeated, "Now Beverley, is there something you want to share with me? I see you have already shared with some members of this class."

This was not going well, so I walked slowly to her desk and placed the bag with the package on it.

"Well, what do we have here?" she said with a nice smile. She removed the package from the bag. "What a lovely gift. Shall I open it, or would you like to?"

Now, I was trapped. With my head down, I activated the mechanism. My teacher screamed and my classmates rolled in laughter, practically falling out of their seats.

When our teacher regained her composure, she said, "That's enough class." The class immediately quieted down.

"Beverley, go back to your seat." I knew she was angry by the sound of her voice.

I guess, if I had to do it all over again, I would have prepared our teacher. I could have said, "This is a joke. A clown is going to jump out." But I said nothing. Not sure if it was because I had misgivings about this teacher. They said she was an alcoholic, but I never saw any indications of that. She was however very messy, with stacks of papers from her classes all around the classroom, which had not been graded. After class, I asked my teacher for my gift. She refused to give it to me. When I got home, I told my mother what happened at school and what I did and ask my mother if she could get the gift back. It was just a joke, and my brothers agreed with me.

Orlando said, "Ah, she's just a killjoy. It's a joke, and she's the one who made Beverley do it."

My mother called for an appointment with the principal regarding my joke gift, which really belonged to her. She went to my school for the appointment. I waited in the hall and watched the vintage Seth Thomas Clock on the wall. I was not allowed to be in the conference. In the end, the principal would not intercede, the gift was not returned to my mother.

I guess the joke was on me.

20

Locker Room

In the fifth grade, my mother took me to LS Ayres department store to be fitted for a training bra. I was not sure why I needed to be fitted, there wasn't much of anything there, but I was excited about this experience, nonetheless. My mother said this is how it's done. An older white lady in the lingerie department took my mother and me into a small beige private dressing room with two Louis-XIV chairs. The lady looked familiar. Yes, 'I remember,' she was the one who fitted my mother for brassieres a number of times.

An appointment was required for this service. I don't think there was any additional cost, other than the cost of the bra. After removing my cotton undershirt and blouse, the fitter looked at my chest, then started pulling my flesh. First, she pulled on the side, then forward, and ultimately placed my tissue (we would have said titties) in the soft fabric of the cotton bra. She told me to bend forward emptying what little tissue I had into the cup of the bra. She told me to put my arms behind my back and fasten the band in back. Even though I was thin, trying to fasten the band in back was hard for me. My arms were just too short. Later at home, I fastened the band in the front, then rotated the bra around my stomach to the back.

I examined my reflection in the mirror and decided that it was just okay. There was a fold of fabric to the side which meant that I did not have enough to fill it out, although, the fitter assured me in no time, it would be filled. I decided not to wait. I stuffed some Kleenex into the cup, and magically, I looked much better.

When the fitting was finished, the lady took us to the sales counter with glass top drawers with an array of panties. My mother pointed to the ones she wanted me to have and the sales lady slid the drawer open, pulling out several pairs. My mother bought me Vanity Fair nylon tailored brief panties in pastel colors, which she also wore. The elastic band of the brief was covered in nylon, so the elastic never touched my skin.

Underwear was important to my mother, because as a pauper child, she did not have any, due to mistreatment by her mean aunt, who never even bought her a dress. My mother grew up wearing potato gunny sacks with slits for the neck and arms. This history, I'm sure, led to my mother getting herself a job here in America. One evening, I heard my parents arguing in their bedroom. The door was open, and I heard my mother asked my father for money to buy underwear. My father, the bread winner, said, "You don't need money to buy panties. There's nothing wrong with the ones you have."

I looked at them from the hallway. My mother was livid! But of course, my father knew what was best, just like the TV series, 'Father Knows Best.' My mother shouted, "You will never tell me when I need panties!" My father looked at her, and my mother's brown eyes, straight and narrow, could have cut him up in pieces.

***

Most mothers in the fifties did not generally work, and certainly not away from home. We had a neighbor who was a hairdresser, who had a very nice shop in the back of their home. Unmarried women were generally schoolteachers, nurses or receptionists. Many still lived with their parents, as well as women who stayed at home to take care of children, their own or others. My mother worked for a family who had young girls, so she knew what to buy, and what services were needed for a girl like me.

***

Later, I asked my mother if I could purchase a cheap padded bra from the S.S. Kresge 5 & 10 Cent store. The prices were much lower, and although the quality was not great, I liked the bra fit better, and I could do it myself. No fitter! A 'five n dime' store, would not have a fitter anyway.

My mother looked at me, probably wondering why this little girl would want to go to a five and dime store to purchase her undergarments, when she provided her daughter a much better option. An option that was shared with women and girls from families with means. But she smiled and said confidently, "Sure Beverley, go ahead. What's the cost?"

***

"I bet you wished you had some of these."

133

My fifth-grade classmate, Agnes, rose majestically, from the bench, Queen of the Locker Room Extravaganza, with her chest extended, but it didn't need to be, because she already had size D cups. Agnes was about five feet four, nicely developed, for which the majority of us needed another year or two to catch up, and she wore tortoiseshell Cat-Eye eyeglasses. We girls sat on the narrow wooden benches in the locker room wearing training bras and cotton Lollypops underpants. (I wore Vanity Fair tailored briefs).

A few girls still wore white undershirts, no bra, with a small pink satin bow at the neckline, while Agnes pranced around the room in lace trimmed, matching Wacoal designer brand hipsters or high cut panties in deep colors like blacks, purples, and reds. Her mom definitely bought her things in a woman's store. They did not have those colors for children's underwear.

But Agnes was quite hilarious, moving about the room, doing her dance moves in her fancy Chantilly lace French underwear. No matter what color her brassieres were, her panties matched: they were a set. Agnes' favorite line was, "I bet you wished you had some of these," as she moved her shoulders back, then up and down, and rounded her bosoms in front of us. We all laughed. She tried to get some of us to join her. Periodically, Olive would. Olive was taller and fuller, but wearing the standard issued (not really, we wore what our mothers bought) white Lollypops.

The two girls moved their hips and Agnes would stick her boobs way out. They did moves to imaginary music or sometimes hummed hit tunes, like "Mr. Lee" by the Bobbettes, pretending to be singing stars with shoulders raised smoothly, arms and hands extended gracefully. We laughed our hearts out. Such a performance! When the gym teacher entered, she said, "What's going on here? It's time to go."

We jumped up and were dressed in seconds in our traditional uniformed blue gym snap-front bloomer gym suits. We pushed the thigh length leg fabric of the bloomer up under the elastic leg band of our panties, as we ran breathlessly to the gym; probably privately wishing, 'we had some of those too.'

The following Monday, gym suits had to be washed and ironed or demerits would be issued during squad inspection, and the entire line would be punished if one suit was not properly cleaned and ironed.

21

Peculiar

My father was very particular. However, peculiar is probably a better word choice, about this new house that we now owned. He did not allow his children to come through the front door. He said that we would ruin the carpet. So, we had to enter through the back door to be let in by our father, during our lunch breaks from school. Many times, he was sound asleep, after all he worked two jobs not counting his ministry work. We would have to run back and forth to the front door and back door, until he heard us. In the winter months, this was uncomfortable as well as annoying, with the snow and ice, and the fall months with the cold rain, we had little time to eat lunch and get back to school.

***

Under my wool coat, I felt sweat creeping down my back and face as we hurried between the two doors, and my body felt limp from the cold. The afternoon frost slapped me in the face, my fingers tingling, and my breathing was heavy from constant running. When my father finally came down to the front door, in his striped pajamas, he ushered us to the back door. We were supposed to understand why this was necessary.

"You can't bring dirt into the house," my father clarified daily. "If you keep walking on the carpet, you will wear it out."

"It's not even good carpeting. It's not wool!" Orlando told us when we were out of our father's earshot. "He's just crazy! Not like we're walking into the living room! There is a big entry hall." The three of us made our continuous paths between the doors, ringing the front door bell each time when we returned. Norman and I didn't say anything. I was too cold and tried to participate in the discussion. My bones dreaded the constant running back and forth, then having to rush to eat lunch.

Sometimes, our father gave Orlando money to run to the corner store to get something for us to eat - lunchmeats, white bread, milk. Otherwise, my father would make us drink sugar and water. He said this was good for us.

"Just drink it! You will be big and strong like me. You see these muscles!" I looked at his muscles, bulging beneath his shirt with veins protruding under his skin. I thought they were like that from his training to be a boxer. I never saw my father drink sugar and water, and he certainly did not have it for a meal.

However, our mother did not agree. I told her, of course. So, he didn't say that anymore.

We were not allowed to sit in the living room, where the only television we had was placed. He said the constant sitting created friction with the fabrics, causing them to wear out quickly. We only sat in the living room when our father was at work, never when he was home. Saturday evenings was the only exception, when he allowed us to watch boxing, his favorite, on the television.

My father sat in his large burgundy velvet tub chair; my mother sat in her green French Provincial chair. Generally, we children sat on the floor next to our mother on big comfy floor pillows she purchased in orange, green, red and gold lame with tassels on the ends. The sofa was on the opposite wall. If you sat there, you could not see the television.

"We can't even sit on this crappy furniture, which he didn't even buy. These are old pieces of furniture from the Marriott Hotel. You see how the velvet is worn out in spots." Orlando said and pointed out the areas to us. "You see how big this shit is. It doesn't even fit our house."

I reminded Orlando, "Mother said you are not to say that word." Orlando eyed me with one brow raised. "Bev, you see how big this stuff is. Why do you think that is?"

By the way, we called our mother, "Mother," because our mother felt that it sounded more American. It took a while for us to remember, but with pinching each other, that helped.

***

I wondered why the furniture was so big. It made the living room and the hallway seem ugly and drab, with those overstuffed dark red velvet pieces.

"He acts like he is doing something for our family, man," Orlando continued. "He ain't doing nothing! What's he saving this old stuff for? Not for us, that's for sure."

We complained to our mother, who was in agreement with us. "Don't worry," she said. "I have a plan. Just wait and be patient."

***

Norman, Eddie and I along with our youngest siblings would go downtown window-shopping every Saturday with our mother. My mother was always looking at furniture and talking to sales reps. She told us to sit down and wait quietly. Then she took us to lunch afterwards, which certainly kept us quiet. We rode a crowded bus and went home the same way, holding on to our many packages. Often during the holidays, we had to stand all the way home, because we were the last stop, and the bus was crowded.

One afternoon, my mother was very excited. She said we had a delivery coming. I wondered what it could be. I could see moisture on my mother's forehead, and she was definitely happy. When the deliverymen came, we watched as they took the used Marriott furniture from the living room and entrance hall and brought in new pieces that actually fit the room.

We were thrilled, but waited for our mother's next move.

"Well," she said. "What do you think?"

We just stared. I'm thinking, 'Daddy's gonna' be really mad.'

"Come on kids," she said enthusiastically. "This is for us. Your Dad can have all the old Marriott stuff he wants; but he better never brings them into this house and say, 'My kids can't sit on them.'"

Then, my mother leaned back and fell into the new sofa, laughing. We jumped in with her screaming and laughing too.

When my father came home from work, looked around the house and said, "Well, what is this?" He was smiling as he looked at the new furniture. Then he said, "D, how are you paying for this?"

My mother looked at him and said, "On Time."

"What?" my father said, still smiling, then his smile turned downward into a frown.

"You better be careful, ya' know. Cha mon, this is not Jamaica," my father said sternly.

I believe my father was worried about the new bills. We were in America with no family, no back-up, and he was struggling to keep a roof over our heads, the family fed, utilities paid, along with doing the things he wanted to do, like starting his own church.

***

About six months later, Norman and I came home from school to see Orlando helping to move furniture with a couple of white men in work clothes who were pulling up the carpet that my father had put in when our family first moved in. There was a large white van parked in front of our house.

When the men were finished, our entire home had been re-carpeted, upstairs and down. It looked really terrific.

We looked at our mother and she said with a big smile and confidence, "Now my children can come through the front door, so there!"

We smiled too, knowing she meant it. I didn't know how my father was going to take this change, because the carpet my mother had removed was in good condition.

"But Mother," we said, and before we could finish the sentence, she interjected, "I don't care what your father says.

I didn't bring my children to America to be second-class citizens."

"Well, alright then!" Orlando shouted. We all started screaming and yelling with excitement.

***

I was nervous, when we came home for lunch with the new carpet in the house. Our father was never in a good mood, and I anticipated he would be furious about this change. We rang the doorbell and listened for our father's heavy steps coming down the stairwell. In his pajamas, he was angry as he looked at us through the front door window. We waited, but he just continued to stare at us, his eyes slightly narrowing. His look was definitely not welcoming.

Ready for the challenge, Orlando spoke up, "Mother said, we can come through the front door. Our father stood there, like petrified wood. I was cold, but we did not move. We stood threesome, with our breaths crystalizing before us. I was ready to return to school and call our mother at work, if our father did not let us in; and I know she would come immediately, but our lunch time would be over. Our father would have a snake, ready to pounce, on his hands, if she had to come and let her children in.

Finally, he let us in. His grey eyes cut through us, but I could tell he was angry for being awakened and having to face the fact his children would be coming through the front door from now on. This was a cardinal sin applied only to us.

Everyone else could use that door, but not his children. He looked defeated, with eyes looking to the floor.

Then he said with irritation as he now looked directly at us, "You better watch yourselves. You're in cahoots with your mother. You just better watch yourselves."

I knew what he meant. Somehow, we would be sorry for taking our mother's side. But I was never sure, what he intended to do about that.

***

My parents continued to play this "who gets what game," over time. If my father placed any restriction that denied his children access or use, my mother would replace the items.

One of the last things my mother replaced was the refrigerator. This had nothing to do with us children, but my parents had an argument, because my mother bought beer home and put it in the refrigerator.

"You can't put beer in this refrigerator," my Dad said.

"Why not?" my mother asked.

"Look D, I am a minister of the gospel. I must lead by example. We can't have any alcoholic beverages in the refrigerator."

I thought, 'Well, what about the Mogen David wine, we drank once a month on Sundays?' I knew if I asked him about that, my father would say, "It's the Blood of Christ, part

143

of the Eucharist, little girl. Haven't I taught you anything?"
But in my mind, I'm thinking, 'It is Still alcohol.'

"I told you before," my mother said confidently, sneering at
him. "You're the preacher. I'm not. God called you, **Not Me**."

"D, you must be sensible. This is my household. You cannot
put beer in my refrigerator."

"What do you mean your refrigerator? The refrigerator
belongs to the family."

"Daphne, I am a man of the 'Cloth.' What would people say
or think?"

My mother looked at him, waited, then said, "I don't give a
damn what they think!" Then, she walked out of the kitchen.

So, my mother did not put any more beer in his refrigerator.
My father was pleased and repeated, "A minister of God does
not have alcohol in his refrigerator. Certainly, you understand
this." He turned toward us, his children, and smiled that
familiar crooked face expression. He believed the matter was
settled. We just watched.

But two months later, my mother bought a new refrigerator
with beer in it.

My mother said an icy-cold beer was refreshing during the summer when it was hot and humid. I thought that it tasted rather bitter, but the kids were not allowed to have one anyway.

Later one muggy summer day, my father was standing in the kitchen drinking a beer, taking deep gulps as he swallowed, really enjoying his refreshing drink.

My mother walked in, with eyes anchored on the bottle in his hand and questioned, "So now you are drinking beer Mr. Preacher man?"

"Ahh mon, I just pulled a beverage out. That's all. How's one to know it's a beer?"

My mother studied his face and said very quietly, "It's written on the bottle, Norm." She turned and walked away, as my father held a Pabst Blue Ribbon beer in his hand.

His kids just looked at him. He was smiling. I thought he wanted to laugh. There was mischief in his eyes, like a boy caught in a lie, but he continued drinking the beer.

22

Party Time

We had our own 5th grade burlesque show, more often than I can remember. We practically fell off the benches with laughter from Agnes' risqué performances, and her ability to draw us, her classmates, into this foolishness. Her imitation was really good. It was amusing, playful, even bemusing. During this was the time, we became more aware of our bodies, and how fragile emotionally we were. We watched her performances, like stick figures in a steamy room, because the majority of us were quite slender, with the exception of four or five who filled out early.

Most of us had a boy in the class we liked, who carried our books and walked us to class, running back so they wouldn't get caught by the tardy bell. I don't recall tardiness being a problem like it can be today; but the sweet blossom of puppy love prevailed.

Sometimes my boyfriend would walk me home after school. At the top of the steps by the maple tree and the black metal street lantern my father installed in our front yard, we would steal a soft kiss. I double checked to be sure that our neighbor was not watching. It was never hungry or sloppy, just special! Then my boyfriend said he had to go and would call me that evening. My heart was pumping in my chest as he ran down the street, carrying my little soul in his khaki pant pocket like marbles. He lived a number of blocks from me.

Occasionally as we got older, in the eighth and ninth grade, a real party was held at one of the boys' home in their basements. We were excited, and we girls talked about the party all week: what we would wear, who we were going to the party with or who we would meet there and hoping our parents would give us permission to go. We made sure all our chores were done, homework, etc., so there would not be questions about whether or not we could attend. Finally, we answered the big questions: Were their parents going to be home? How were we getting back home? We really tried to negotiate the time our parents wanted us back home, and when we wanted to be back.

I was pretty lucky because I had two older brothers who would walk me to the party and come back to walk me home. My girlfriends without brothers usually got permission to go with me, and my brothers. Norman was friends with my friends, so he had permission to go as well.

When the party started, all was well. The boy's parents, and other parents who stayed a little while chitchatting with the homeowner, greeted us. There were soda bottles neatly stacked and chilled in a cooler and potato chips in a bowl on a card table. The music was going strong. The "Twist," by Chubby Checker would lead off, and our bodies were twisting, as we had laughed and exaggerated our hips while alternating lifting our legs, just like Chubby did, to the popular hit. Such great fun, with the heat radiating from our bodies sifting off into the evening. My mother's Chanel No 5, now dissipating as well, rolling off with the sweat that trickled down behind my ears and my back. My mother usually left her crystal perfume bottle on her mahogany dresser top. I picked up the perfume and placed a dab in back of my ears and on the pulse of my wrist (that's where the commercial said the perfume would be the most effective) before I left home, feeling quite grown up.

The guys generally wore the smell of "Old Spice," cologne (which our fathers' had, along with a little sweat probably from dancing; but we were having such fun, no one really cared. Eventually one of the boys would turn off the fluorescent ceiling lights and play slow songs like "Tears on My Pillow" or "Goodnight Sweetheart, Goodnight." The basement amplified our voices, and you would have thought that we were a large Episcopal chorus with a pipe organ behind our singing. We sang along to the funny songs too like 'Chantilly Lace' - "Chantilly Lace and a pretty face, and a ponytail hanging down. A giggle and a talk, makes the world go round...." "The Purple people Eater...," was another favorite – "It was a One Eyed One Horned Flying Purple People...."

Oh, we were happy! You wanted to be sure you were with your boyfriend on the special slinky numbers, not just some guy asking you to dance. You would lean into your boyfriend and he rolled his hips slowly into you.

The heat rose, penetrating every inch of our bodies and the room. Sweat rolled down my face, and my boyfriend's cheek touching my own intensified the heat in my body. I thought momentarily about my hair as the side of his warm face pressed against my freshly straightened and curled hairdo, parted to the side and slightly draped across my forehead. We did not have our hair permed with those kits that came out later, in those days. Everything was natural, and I mean really natural. My hair was soft, (not the manageable kind) and it could put up quite a fuss! So, I released my hand from my partner, ever so gently, trying not to disrupt our special time; but knowing my hair would be a total mess, I had to try.

It never failed, just when you were feeling so special, lights out, your eyes closed, your mind and body in a dreamy world of touch, sound and smells, you would hear a muscle of confusion. When I opened my eyes, the commotion was even louder.

"What's going on down here? Who turned out the lights?"
"Ah Mom, it's no big deal."
"I told you the lights stay on. Who do you think is in charge here?"

The brightness in the room was overwhelming, and I felt exposed, like all my clothes had been removed. My eyes kept blinking like venetian blinds flashing up and down on a string. As my vision adjusted, I saw the off-white ceiling

149

acoustical tiles, beige walls, brown banister railing leading upstairs with a number of the boys heading up as well, grabbing sodas on the way.

By this time, the girls were lined up outside the restroom door. Only two or three girls can get in there at a time, well - not really, but we all grew up together sharing the locker room, so it did not matter. When I saw my hair, I could not believe it. A big mass of matted hair! What happened to my hairdo? I didn't have a comb, so I took my fingers and ran them through my hair, trying to curl a finger wave. 'Why would anyone be attracted to me?' I thought. I really looked bad. I should correct myself and say, 'My hair really looked bad. I mean really bad!' My clothes and shoes, however, still looked pretty good."

I heard Norman calling for me, so I asked my girlfriend for a bobby pin, and clipped my top hair off to the side. Outside the house, my boyfriend walked with me for a little while. However, his mother and aunt were there to walk him home, so he could only walk me to the corner. I could see his mother from a distance. I had seen her before at school. She was tall and very attractive. She could have been a model. She looked a lot younger than my mother. My friend was an only child. I did not want her to see my hair, although my boyfriend did not seem to mind. I walked home with my brother and a couple of his buddies, and my girlfriends. We girls walked behind them, with my brother saying from time to time, "Okay Carol, here's your pad."

We all marveled at the fun we had as we walked home that evening. It was dark, but there was a streetlight at every corner.

"Boy, when his Mom turned the lights on, that ruined everything," Norman's buddy said. "Yeah!" my brother said. "But we still had a good time though."

My friends and I smiled to ourselves. No one could really see our faces in the dark; but we had to agree, it was a nice party.

23

Clara

Clara and I were probably in the seventh or eighth grade when we met. We didn't attend the same school, nor did we live in the same neighborhood. Clara was a very nice person and a good buddy. We did a lot of musical events together, and her parents often provided transportation for me to rehearsals and concerts. We both played viola in the Indianapolis City Orchestra. Sometimes, the sectional rehearsals were held at a local church. All the full rehearsals were held in a large gymnasium. These locations were rotated around the city.

I can't remember if Clara's viola was the same size as mine, because my viola was way too big for me. My father said I would grow into it. But at least it was mine.

We were about the same age, but you would never have known it, because Clara was so tall in the seventh and eighth grades. Clara had already surpassed 7 feet. She was indeed a big girl, not skinny like me. I looked like an elementary kid next to Clara. She stood strong and sturdy with smooth brown skin. She had really large feet, which fit her body of course, but was a little clumsy at times. She wore custom made shoes, leather ones like Buster Browns with a single strap across the instep.

Clara's parents were tall as well. Her father was about 6'9" and her mother was easily 6'5." They had professional jobs, I assumed, because they always had business suits on. Her mother wore a white button front blouse under her suit with a small velvet tie at the neckline.

Years later, Clara was mentioned in the Guinness Book of World records. I lost touch with her after high school. I learned that she died in her twenties. She was, however, a giant in spirit, in mind and body. What a special girl, and special friend.

24

Jim Crow

As children, we were not aware of the indignities our parents faced, and my father probably thought it didn't apply to him anyway. He was initially a Jamaican national, who later became a naturalized citizen. As children, we just ran around and played having a good time, that is after we finished our chores so my father wouldn't be angry. It was later I realized that there were major differences in our lives and in the lives of other people, particularly people who did not look like us, white people.

Signs were clearly posted everywhere, letting us (Negroes) know our place. "Whites Only," "Colored Only," "Negroes Only," signs were on restaurants, restrooms, buses, as well as implied in neighborhoods, churches and schools. The only way out of segregated schools was to test out, which was also part of Jim Crow. Everything that was labeled "colored" was generally inferior, and certainly wasn't maintained. You would not want to use that facility.

As a child, all I really cared about was going to the amusement park. It looked like so much fun from the outside. I saw white children and their parents lined up at the gate or in the park having a wonderful time. I wanted to be like them. My father had the money. He worked three jobs, after all. It wasn't until the Civil Rights Act of 1964 that the amusement park was open to all the residents of Indianapolis, Indiana; not just for "Whites Only!"

By then, I had a boyfriend who took me to the park a couple of times in the evening as the sun was setting. We rode many rides, but one of my favorites was going through this labyrinth of water in what was called by teenagers 'the Love tunnel.' It was almost pitch black as we slowly journeyed through the water with a leather seatbelt strapping the two of us together. Soft music was playing, and images were glowing in the stage props along the way. I rested my head on boyfriend's shoulders, and he gently kissed me. 'Puppy love,' they called it.

The other place I thought I wanted to go was to the swimming pool. There were none near my home, other than "Whites Only" facilities. We had an Olympic size pool at my high school, but you had to be enrolled in swimming class to use it. No one used it after school or on the weekends, other than the swim team. When my mother got her own car, she took us to another location probably forty-five minutes from our home in congested traffic. We were allowed to swim there; but I quickly realized that swimming would not be for me, because of my hair. In spite of the tight- fitting rubberized swimming cap I wore, when I got out of the water, my hair was a mess, sopping wet from back to front. It was so frustrating and discouraging when I looked in the mirror and saw my reflection. I carried a soft hat, like a Kaminsky with a wide brim and wore a small silk scarf underneath the hat where I wrapped my hair.

***

In junior high school, we prepared for the Stanford Achievement Tests and the Iowa Test of Basic Skills every year. This was the criteria used to determine what high school you went to. Now I assumed all the students in the high school were required to meet the grade level mastery or above on those tests. Then I questioned to myself, 'What if only the students from minority junior high schools, 'Separate but Equal' schools, were tested?' 'Test taking' was big business, with all of these booklets wrapped in plastic, including practice tests, answer sheets, #2 pencils and worksheets; all materials had to be counted and accounted for. Everyone took those tests or similar ones.

Most of the Black children went to Crispus Attucks High School, named for the first man who died in the Boston Massacre, and he was African American. A percentage went to Shortridge High School, a college prep school and the remainder attended the massive Arsenal Technical High School. Orlando attended Crispus Attucks. I'm sure he didn't do well on the test, because he wanted to go with his friends to Attucks. They probably didn't even go to school on the days of testing. They, including my brother, were just so cavalier about school. Seemingly, his friends just wanted to hang out on the street corner. The rest of the children in my family attended Shortridge High School based on our scores.

156

At the time, many minority families also selected Crispus Attucks, because it was fully funded, and their students went on to colleges as well, becoming doctors, lawyers and teachers.

At Shortridge, you had to purchase your own books, an expense my father willingly paid for each of his children. It was bad when they changed editions, and you had to buy new books, which were costly. For some of the general classes, Norman would give his books to me and when the semester was over, I sold it back to the bookstore and we shared the little profit. The books were yours and you could sell them back to the bookstore if they were in good condition or keep them. Your choice! Norman and I kept the money, a lot less than what you paid for the book, but you got a little something back. We never gave the money back to our father. Well, he never asked for it anyway! He probably didn't know we could sell them back, and that we did.

As for musical instruments, you paid for your own or rented one. My father bought my viola when I was in junior high.

In the summer of 1966 after my first year of college, I wanted to take my new boyfriend, now my husband Clarence to the amusement park I was not allowed to visit as a child, because of the color of my skin. My good memories were shattered. The place was run down, no longer the oasis in the heart of the city, with manicured lawns and cultivated flowers. It was slowly becoming a ruin, like what some white people thought of us. They believed we ruined their neighborhoods, their parks, their restrooms, restaurants, the places that were home to them, never to be shared with us. We weren't there by invitation, so the facility did not deserve to be kept up for sharing with colored people. No one could legislate bringing the masses together for the common good. Whose common good were you interested in anyway. There were always at least two.

25

Algebra

It was her shoes that I remember most; leather hard soled with thinly waxed laces, in three colors: a black pair, a brown pair, and a camel-colored pair. Regardless of the color, each pair was exactly the same. Highly polished, you could probably see your face in them. These shoes belonged to my Algebra II teacher. She had also been my Algebra I teacher. Camel colored cotton socks complimented her shoes, and at wintertime, long woolen stockings extended far above her knee. As her shoes dictated, her dresses were simple - shirt-waist dresses, which we could easily make in our junior high school Home Economics' class, in a heavier broadcloth fabric. They were starched to perfection and could probably stand up on their own. The dresses looked like what a cafeteria worker would wear, except my teacher's dresses were in deep colors – tans, and navy blues. Once in a while she wore a collared white blouse trimmed in lace, with a camel-colored cardigan sweater and a straight or sometimes pleated skirt.

The incongruence was great. She was probably in her early forties, but her selection of clothing was for a much older woman.

This was my second year of high school, in the tenth grade, and I still found my algebra teacher intimidating. She was businesslike, slightly stocky, but equally proportioned and fully curved. She had black wavy hair, frizz-free, shiny, and always pulled tightly in a low chignon bun at the back of her neck, neatly coifed. Her skin was a coffee with cream color. Her face was round and full and she wore a little foundation and face-powder. She had perfectly arched eyebrows, and thin lips with red lipstick.

When she walked past my desk, I heard a swishing sound, probably made by her satin slip rubbing against the bones of her girdle, which all women wore for modesty and to pull in those stomachs, and keep your body from shaking, particularly your behind. On Sundays for church, young girls wore them too, and I was among those numbers. Frequently, I had to go to the restroom to pull that girdle down. I wore the brief girdle. My mother wore the thigh length girdle, as did most women. My mother's girdle had a zipper on one side and an extended thick elastic band for slenderizing the waist. Sometimes, I would help my mother get into it, before church. However, my little girdle would ride up into my crotch, and it was most uncomfortable. I could not wait to pull all that elastic down. I was thin and really did not need a girdle, but that was the expectation, my right of passage into womanhood.

Our classroom was always super quiet, with all heads bent forward, in the thirty-five or so seats, working on assignments. Our teacher walked up and down the aisles quietly, pausing momentarily at the individual desks, looking over assignments. She made comments as necessary. This one time, I was particularly nervous. I did not want her to stop by my desk, examine my work and ask me to explain why I had done it that way. My heart was beating like a drum in my chest as I sensed her approach.

My mind said, 'Please, please don't stop at my desk. Just keep going. Please! I don't want any help.' The reality was I didn't want her to question me. I always did well on my tests, my operations in order, but I could not explain how I got the answer; but more often than not, they were right. My mind worked intuitively without me.

Even with two years as my algebra teacher, I was still not comfortable with her. However, I admit, I was fairly good in Algebra.

***

It was in geometry that I was terrible. I had a different teacher. She must have been in her eighties, very tiny, humped shouldered thin white lady. She looked like someone's great, great, grandmother, with this soft little voice, and baby soft silky hair. You could see her scalp through her hair. I strained every day to hear what she said. If a classmate sneezed or cough, FORGET It! I could not hear a word she said.

***

I heard two years before, my teacher's husband, a retired military man, died of natural causes. Older students said, she was different after that. However, she was still always punctual, greeted you at the door with a nod as you walked by; although it was clear to me, that this was a woman who did not seem approachable. Other than a question about algebra, I would never have approached her on any other topic, not even if I had menstrual cramps and wanted to go to the nurse's office.

One morning, the teacher next door opened our classroom door to let us in. This was most unusual, because our teacher was never absent and God forbid, she would ever be late. The tardy bell rang at 8:00 am. Our class was busy, quietly reviewing the homework from the night before. The door was left open in case we needed the teacher next door for assistance. The halls were always empty and quiet once the tardy bell rang. We never goofed off in class, not even a note was passed. Our teacher would not permit it. There was a presence about her that said, "Do Not Mess with Me." She allowed us to ask questions at the beginning of class regarding our homework, and periodically, she had classmates come up to the chalk board to demonstrate how they had solved the problem. She stood to the side of the blackboard, with a long wooden pointer with a black rubber tip, which she tapped on the problem (assigned from the textbook) for emphasis.

I had not even noticed our teacher was still not there. I just assumed she had come in quietly while we were working. It was long after 8:15 a.m., and the class was busy with our individual assignments, when our school principal walked in. I looked up, the Seth Thomas clock on the wall behind him said 8:22 a.m. He was a tall white man, probably 6'2" or 4", with thinning hair, and soft eyes. His suit jacket looked a little large on him, as if he had lost some weight, but it was neatly pressed.

"Students, I want to share with you some information about your teacher." He certainly had our attention as we stared at him and glimpsed at each other.

He went on to tell us our teacher had been found dead in her car that morning. I immediately thought someone had been lying in wait for her and killed her. The principal continued. The car was parked in the garage of their home. Her car was running, and the doors were locked with windows rolled up. He said the police were investigating her case as a possible suicide.

Now, we were speechless. "What about her son," we asked. He was about our age, 17 years old or so.

Her son had apparently left earlier on the school bus and was now just being notified by law enforcement.

I felt like I had been punched in the chest, as I felt bile moving up my system and thought I was going to be sick. Once my stomach settled, I thought, 'How could she do this to her son? Didn't she know that her son needed her? How could she take her own life? Why, why? It was not right. She was selfish to do this to her son.' Sure, I reflected, she was saddened after the death of her husband; but she had a son to live for. My mother had depression too, but she always said, "I live for my children."

The principal continued saying we would have a substitute teacher until a permanent teacher was found. He told us that he was sure that there would be more information in the newspapers, and for us to look it up and read about our teacher's situation. In the meantime, he reminded us that our teacher genuinely cared about us and wanted us to be successful; and he did not want us to add to the tragedy. "Be the best student you can be. That is what your teacher wanted. That is what she expected."

My heart was heavy. I never really got to know my teacher, but I depended on her to help me understand what I was doing in Algebra. I followed her line of thinking, and never questioned. I never asked her how was her day? Never noticed she was suffering in any way! Only once in a while she might mention her son, with a big smile, if we asked about him. He had to be brave now, like his father, the military man.

Walking home with Norman after school, the word had spread about my teacher. Norman said she died from carbon monoxide poisoning. I wasn't sure what that was; so, Norman explained it too me. I didn't realize you could sit in a car and die, if you had the motor on, in some enclosed environment. We were always sitting in the car with the motor on, waiting on someone in the family who forgot something. Granted, we were parked on the street, not in a garage.

***

You would think by now, I could reconcile what my teacher did. Show some empathy for the pain she was feeling right there in front of me; but I can't let go. I can't forgive her for willingly leaving her son at such an age.

26

Growing Up

Indianapolis, like so many other cities across the nation, embraced Jim Crow Laws and made it clear Black folks could not exercise their constitutional rights and enjoy the same freedoms and privileges as white people. Within a silence which permeated the city, it seemed that it was a nice place to live, if you didn't know better. Signs dictated the fabric of race relations from restrooms to schools, and restaurants to miscegenation; but Indiana was also part of the Bible Belt with churches on every other corner, Christian and Protestant fundamentalist abound, yet frankly, no one talked about sex.

Other than menstrual cycles for girls and wet dreams for boys discussed in school health classes, that was it. Yet evidence was everywhere about sex. Girls were sent away to homes of relatives until their babies were born. Married women with men coming home from the Korean War hid their children with other families. Service men never mentioned, if they even knew, offspring in faraway places, but we saw their progeny on TV reels, newspapers and in the *Weekly Readers* at school. Children grew up playing alongside cousins, only to find out, they were not cousins, and their aunt was actually their mother. Even in church it was rumored one of the ministers was having an affair with a member and she was pregnant. She had a baby, and no one said a word, not openly that is. Later, they got married.

In the fifth grade, my mother brought me pamphlets about menstruation, sex, how babies were born, birth control, and a host of other interesting topics. She probably got them at the doctor's office or Planned Parenthood Health Center where my mother went to help control the size of her family, after her fifth child was born. These readings were medically analytical as well as anatomically correct, rather than sensual. They definitely were not Harlequin Romances, which some of the kids read, even though the paperbacks were old copies, shabby and torn.

But these new pamphlets held my interest. Many times, while sitting alone on the front porch's wooden green swing, I would pull out my pamphlets, one by one. I kept them in a plastic satchel with a zip lock on top. They had about fifteen to twenty 6'x 9"- pages each, I read them, and looked carefully at the drawings. This added a lot of interest for summer reading, other than Edgar Allen Poe's *The Raven,* or George Elliot's poor *Silas Marner* or *Great Expectation* by Charles Dickens; but I must admit I enjoyed reading about Pip and Estelle. They were about my age.

***

My freshman year of high school, they had four different lunch schedules. This was quite unusual for me and stressful. With my music (symphony) schedule, I did not have lunch with my friends. The first day of fall semester, I wondered around the massive lunchroom with large blond wooden tables and matching chairs, trying to find a place to sit, which was truly intimidating. My lunch tray rested on top of my books. My wallet was in my leather purse with the long strap that hung over my shoulder. I was getting anxious, and my arms were getting tired, when I heard a girl say,

"Hey, join us over here." She appeared to be older than me.

I looked over to see if she was actually talking to me, the younger, plain and skinny girl. The lunch table length, about three, six-foot tables joined together, was crowded with older pretty girls, both Black and white. Books and jackets were piled everywhere. But for seniors and juniors, everyone respected their space. They were confident.

'Certainly, she could not be talking to me,' I thought.

But the girl continued, "Come on over. We can move down and make space. This place is really crowded at lunch."

I could not believe she was talking to me with a nice smile and pretty hair, good hair they called it back then. She gestured, so I followed her lead. I ended up eating lunch with these girls over time, not just my freshman year, but other years as well. Each year, the girls who were left after graduation added younger girls, like I had been when they invited me to join their group.

We were not isolated from the guys. They had their own tables; they would run over, two or three at a time and say

168

something to one of the girls or to the table, smile and then returned to their friends. These girls were popular, and I knew it. I learned some of the girls were Student Body officers, and all of the girls belonged to Girls League, elected from their Homerooms, plus members of the Honor Roll, National Honor Society, and on the Yearbook and daily newsletter staff.

I found the company of these older girls quite interesting. I listened mostly because they had so much to say, and their conversations included far more experience than I had. One day the discussion was about babies. I was surprised to learn, that one of the girls had a baby and just returned to school that fall. She was so pretty and petite, wore lovely clothes, and had gorgeous eyes and hair. In spite of the loud and hectic sounds of the cafeteria, and guys laughing their heads off nearby, I could hear her well. I sat only three seats away from her. She started telling us about her mysterious illness which turned into a pregnancy. She said that she had gotten the sperm from a toilet seat. She told us to be very careful if you went into a public restroom where men also used the facility, because sperm could be waiting for you, and enter your vagina when you least suspected.

I listened and weighed on her every word. After all, she had been through this horrible experience and she wanted us to be safe. She really cared about us, and she just recently met me. I had no idea a pregnancy could occur like that. I did not dare say anything, because 'What did I know anyway?' I vowed not to set my skinny butt down on any public toilet seat.

Months later after much apprehension about going to public restrooms and straining my knees so my butt would not touch a strange toilet seat, I asked my mother if such a pregnancy could be possible.

My mother said, "No Beverley, you should know better." She also said the girl lied to us to cover her own shame and embarrassment regarding an unwanted pregnancy. "And where is the baby?" my mother asked. "Who is taking care of it? Did she give her child up for adoption?"

I stood speechless. I could not answer a single question. I thought maybe her mother or grandmother was taking care of the baby. But I never asked. It just didn't seem my place to ask. After all, I really did not know this girl. I didn't even know you could have a baby and return to school. All of this was new to me.

"But Mother," I said, "Couldn't this be possible? She really wanted us to be very careful. She was so nice."

"No," my mother repeated. "Don't let anyone tell you such foolishness. You've been reading those pamphlets I gave you for years. I see you reading them. They are **not fairytales**," my mother emphasized.

So, I sat back wondering about my new lunch mate, as my mother went to cook dinner. My new friend must have been so frightened and embarrassed to have concocted such a story; but she seemed so sincere, so caring. I think she really believed that was how it happened.

On the other hand, my level of ignorance continued. I said to myself, 'My mother is from Jamaica. Maybe things are different there.' So, I continued anchoring my butt over public toilet seats for a while longer, not wanting to take any chances. Sperm Awaits! SUCH A FOOL, I was!

Each time I saw my new friend at lunch, I wondered about her. I also wondered why none of her friends challenged her. Could they all be in on the secret, and I was the only fool in the crowd? Did they laugh when I was not around? Somehow, I thought not.

I believed they loved her and wanted to spare her any additional hurt or humiliation; because it was clear, she was emotionally devastated. I wondered if her child was growing up as her baby sister or brother.

27

Black Beauty

Walking hurriedly across the Terrazzo floors of the art wing at the high school, I heard a boy yell, "Black Beauty, wait up!" I knew he was not talking to me, as I stiffen. I would never answer to such a name.

In high school, Black heritage was not popular. Black was not considered beautiful. It was not until I went to college that a major cultural revolution exploded. We actually wore our hair natural and used Afro Picks. I remembered in 1968, we enthusiastically danced to James Brown's song, "I'm Black and I'm Proud," with sweat running down our backs, in dance halls on campus.

***

But this was high school: I looked up when I heard his voice. 'How dare he use such a derogatory name, in full view and hearing of anyone present in the hall,' I thought. Then I saw a girl coming towards me. I blinked my eyes as the sun infused vintage hall of the art gallery required, when I saw her. I was stunned.

Taught not to stare, which was impolite, I could not help it.

This girl was probably six feet tall, slim, with a graceful neckline and long black shiny hair past her shoulders. Reducing my steps, I watched as she slowed to a stop to the boy's request. Her skin was blue black, soft like silk, and she was stunningly beautiful. Her skin looked like light reflecting off a quiet deep blue lake, with diamonds floating on the surface.

She was indeed a unique human specimen; I never saw her before, seemingly out of place in this gothic, art deco gallery. Maybe, I was the one out of place and she was simply an extension of the art shared in that wonderful space. Her voice was soft, higher in tone than I expected, yet surprisingly pleasing to hear, no foreign accent denoted. Her facial features were finely sculptured, with small lips as dark as her skin, yet they looked moist, and soft as a powder puff.

I slowed down as she had, avoiding our befalling the same spot at the same time; but I could not take my eyes off her. "Black Beauty," students called this girl, and it was definitely not a put-down, or an insult. It was instead, a tribute to a living mortal who was splendidly gorgeous, and outrageously different, who gave us a moment in time to reflect on who we were. I wondered if she was a Watusi? I saw pictures in Look Magazine of this tribe moving gracefully through the jungle brush, towering above the tall grasses. The people were striking to look at: slim, graceful and tall.

"Black Beauty," here in America and England was the story of a horse I remembered reading in junior high. It told the adventures and hardships of this horse, a working horse, yet also the kindness and understanding of this horse by those he came in contact with, was compelling. That is where this name came from, I would think. The story has been around for ages, triumphing the challenges of this thoroughbred. It was later developed into a series for television, *The Adventures of Black Beauty*. I remember the magnificent animal and enjoyed the chronicles of its life.

***

In high school, I realized students have an unadorned way of seeing the world more clearly. That is why they associated this name with this beautiful young girl. I heard other students who were friends call her "Black Beauty," even Norman did so. Each time I heard her name called, I looked up and waited to see this special girl pass by. I no longer stared at her, because I could visualize in my head her composition, her delicate bone structure, and distinctive beauty. Was she African or East Indian? I didn't know. Yet, she was unquestionably a stout-hearted soul standing confidently among us. We, on the other hand, were the plain grasses yielding to the wind, touching the ground, and slapping each other as she passed.

28

4H

I was 15 years old when my Home Economics teacher told the class about the 4-H competition in which you could compete in a number of categories. I was interested in the sewing. It sounded like it would be a fun project for the summer. I was confident that I could compete, because sewing was such an integral part of my life. My father was a tailor who made men's suits and women's garments. My grandmother and my aunt were also seamstresses. They made my mother's wedding gown.

The following Saturday my mother and I went downtown to shop for fabrics for my project. We selected a pattern and a soft peach polished cotton fabric. The pattern was in a current style, popular with women and girls. It was a typical shirt waist dress with gathered skirt, but what made it special was that it had ruffles down the front, a collar, and set- in three quarters of a length sleeves with ruffles. The pattern also called for insets under the arms to reduce the fabric tension when you raised you them. A three-inch fabric covered belt and buckle with eyelets were also required, along with a hem four inches in depth. I was so excited.

I laid the fabric with the pattern out on the dining room table, knowing that each day I had to stack the pieces up, because the family ate dinner there. However, with the pieces cut, it took up less space. The closer I was to finishing the project, the more euphoric I became, until it was time to turn it in.

More than a month passed during the time I completed the project. One day at the end of school the teacher asked me to come to her desk, just as the dismissal bell rang. I watched my fellow students leave, before I approach the teacher's desk. Needless to say, I was nervous. This could be one of the biggest days of my life! When I approached the desk, the teacher was reluctant to look at me, even though we had developed a long friendship. She had also been my junior high Home Economics teacher before she transferred to the high school.

I waited, sensing that something was wrong. Then she said solemnly, "Your dress was disqualified." Now she looked at me as a single tear escaped, running down her cheek.

I felt frantic. 'There must be some mistake,' I thought.

"Why?" I finally asked. I didn't cry. Just waited!

She took a deep breath and continued, "A panel of judges concluded that the garment could not have been made by a student."

I just stared at her, as I registered what she was saying. 'They concluded I was the dishonest one.' I picked up my books and walked out, with my teacher watching me. I am thinking to myself, 'Couldn't she have vouched for me. Told them what an excellent student I was. Wouldn't they have believed her?'

I vowed I would never enter another 4H competition. It certainly was not worth my calculations of time and energy.

Nearing the last day of school, my teacher announced that students were being considered for red and blue place ribbons at the Indiana State fair. They were so happy, and I was so deflated. 'One of those awards should have been mine,' I thought. 'The judges stole it from me.'

I went on to wear that lovely dress to my sweet sixteen surprise birthday party. It looked just lovely and I felt really good wearing it. I continued to sew clothes for my mother and for myself over those years. Later when I was in college, I made a man's walking suit, for Clarence, who is now my husband.

29

Carrie

In the hallway outside of the hospital waiting room, my brother Norman stood lifeless, like a statue, eyes darkened and blank. I stood next to him, providing no comfort, just someone who loved him nearby. No one asked us to move as the flurry of activities around us seemed urgent and prophetic. I know Norman was wondering how this happened. He always played the role of a Casanova, with girls seemingly coming out of the woodwork to be with him. Carrie was such a girl. Always waiting for him, even though she saw him with other girls.

Over the months, I watched the two of them together - Norman carrying Carrie's books; walking her to class; giving her a big wave as she went in, before he took off running, trying not to be late for his own class; or walking her home after school, like they were savoring every moment. She looked quite content, a soft smile on her face, as she strolled along with my brother at her side. And of course, Norman spent hours on the telephone with Carrie each night, when he should have been studying, but my mother did not know. I stayed a good distance away, not teasing him, as I normally did; because Norman shared with me Carrie was pregnant. He did not know what to do; but at least he told our mother. My father never knew.

Carrie was certainly nice enough, on the shorter side, probably 5' or so, small in frame like me, and she pursued my brother with a crushing relevance. Norman was happy-go-lucky, never taking life seriously. He just wanted to play alley basketball, and mess around with girls; but Carrie was ready for a serious life partner.

When our mother dropped us off at high school, Norman and his buddies quietly swaggered to one of the several back doors and cut classes, most of the morning. He liked his shop class and sports class in the afternoon, so he came back. Norman had a lot of growing up to do and had plenty of time to do that. I think he really enjoyed his childhood, particularly his teenage years with his 'side-kicks.'

***

Our mother met us in the hall of the hospital that evening. She saw Carrie in the ward and said she didn't look good. She was swollen and on a ventilator. My mother and I looked at each other, while Norman stared at the floor. Shortly afterwards, Carrie's father, a small thin man, approached us in the hall.

"I don't know what to say. I'm lost. My baby might be dying. We were in the car together. I didn't even see the car that hit us, until it was too late. But I'm standing here, and Carrie might be taken from me."

My mother extended some words of comfort, but Norman and I said nothing. Norman rarely looked up. It was last night, when my brother received a call from Carrie's younger sister. She said Carrie and her father were involved in a car accident. They were the only two in the car. Carrie in the passenger seat was ejected from the vehicle.

I saw Carrie's mother in the distance, walking towards us. I knew this was her, because she always stood at the front door when Carrie came home from school, and waved to us, while letting Carrie in. She was short, barely 5 feet, and on the plump side. My mother acknowledged her with the movement of her head. Neither woman spoke nor smiled. Carrie's mom stressed over the condition of her daughter, and my mother was probably grateful it wasn't her child.

When Carrie's parents walked away, my mother asked Norman, if he wanted to see her. Norman said nothing. I said that I would go, and so I followed my mother into the hospital ward crowded with patients in similar condition as Carrie.

I was overwhelmed by the numbers of patients, the permeating smell of alcohol and meds, the sound of bells, beeps and infrasonic sounds going off, clear plastic containers with tubes dripping into the patient's veins, and lights in red, blue, white and green, coming from the individual monitors, flashing from the triage stations.

The emergency wing was open for all. No privacy curtains separating the beds. The bodies of all these patients were exposed to doctors, nurses, orderlies, cafeteria workers, and visitors. I stood next to Carrie's body. She was unconscious, her face strangely puffed-up and bruised with plastic tubing going up her nostrils. Beneath her white bed blanket, her bloated chest moved up and down slowly while clear fluids from an IV bag dripped like water sliding off a keg of ice into her veins. I looked at her stomach and it was barely moving. 'No one said anything about the baby,' I kept thinking. 'Something must be wrong,' as a nervousness took over me, and my stomach now churned.

***

I remember when my mother's friend lost her unborn baby and husband in a car accident. She was the only survivor. I was, however, surprised to see this tiny baby, about 8 months (premature), in a little bitty casket at the service. The infant was placed in the larger casket next to her father's lower leg. So sad, I remembered, but father and daughter looked at peace, just like they were sleeping.

***

When my mother and I walked away, I asked quietly, "What about the baby? Where is it? Are they going to induce labor?" They had done this when my mother had her last child. "Did the baby survive?"

My mother said nothing, as we continued walking the long corridor, and people flashed by us in a whirlwind of activities. My mother stopped and moved to the side. Looked at me with such intensity that I was frightened. Then she said simply, "There was no baby."

181

I was stunned. "No baby?" I questioned, but Carrie had a large stomach, wore big tops to school, I am thinking. They looked like maternity tops to me. She looked pregnant. What kind of trick is this? Why would her parents have gone along with this mean joke?

My mother, wiped the moisture from her forehead, with her arm, then repeated without blinking, but with solace, "There was no baby."

***

Now I realized why the two women, Carrie's mother and my mother, barely acknowledged each other earlier. They both bore the emptiness of "There was no baby." My mother probably pained by what Norman had been through, for naught; and Carrie's mother, whether or not she knew before, certainly knew that truth now. The concealment exposed.

***

Carrie died the next day, never returning to consciousness. Norman, our mother and I went to the funeral. I was sorry that Carrie's life ended this way, so tragically; but I was also angry with her for perpetuating this lie. My God, what was she doing, stuffing her stomach with towels as she dreamed of a life with my brother, when she had major flaws? I didn't know if she was mentally ill, or what, or if she just wanted so badly to be pregnant. But there was no mention of a baby in the funeral program, and judging by the size of Carrie's stomach, the baby would have been about seven to eight months old. Needless to say, there was not an infant sized casket at the service.

***

Norman never mentioned the baby. In fact, Norman said very little if anything. I just assumed he knew there was no baby, and there was never one. If he did know, the weight of Carrie's deception must have figuratively thrown him to the ground. Did he grieve for the baby that never was? I can't answer that. It just did not seem like my place to have this discussion with him; and if he thought Carrie was so nice, it was not my position to disarm him. On the other hand, if my brother was able to link her behavior with mental illness, neither of us was mature enough nor knowledgeable enough to handle that information either.

***

We never talked about Carrie, nor did I talk with my mother about her. I guess I was just plain speechless, when my mother told me, "There was No Baby!' I could not believe it and I still do not believe it; yet all the evidence supported my mother's words. This was really baffling to me. 'Why would Carrie do this? Why?' Whatever the reason, she took the answer with her in death.

30

Talent Show

Once a year, our high school sponsored a talent show after school at 5:00 p.m. After getting permission, Norman and I bought tickets and met in the gymnasium. The gym was extraordinarily large with a ceiling height that surpassed a three-story building. Sounds echoed off the walls, giving one the feeling of being in a cave.

On each level of the gym, from the first to the third floor, students entered and departed through multiple double doors. Norman and his buddies agreed to meet me and a couple of my friends, on the third level, which was not far from the music rooms.

Norman and I were excited about attending the Talent Show, sitting high above all the pandemonium below was the perfect place to be, because the first two levels filled rapidly.

On the upper level, members of the football team and basketball team trickled in quietly after practice. I dated two members of the basketball team, not at the same time of course, but after the first guy graduated. I liked their heights and firm conditioned bodies. I always felt little, (I probably weighed 98 pounds when I graduated from high school.) so, it was nice to look up to these gentle giants and feel like I was on equal footing, and they treated me like I was special.

Students were laughing and yelling, while the Assistant Principal tried to get the crowd under control, so the show could start. Each group or individual, who came forward to perform, was booed and heckled. Granted, they were not really good, but at least they tried. During school day assemblies held in Mills Hall, unruly behavior like this would not be tolerated. Each class was assigned seats, escorted by their teacher to the event, and remained until dismissed by the principal. None, of these shenanigans, would be permitted.

But after school, they allowed us to be silly and act like kids having fun. Boos and jeering continued, even as a very small frame girl, about 5' 1" tall stepped to the podium to sing a cappella. No band or piano player accompanied her. This would not go well, I thought. Now the crowd really went wild, with cow calls, whistles and just plain rudeness. I saw this girl before, but Norman knew her. "Hey, that's Eve," he said.

Eve held the mike to her mouth and started belting out "Gee whiz, look at his eyes; Gee whiz, how they hypnotize; He's got everything a girl could want; Man, oh, man, what a prize! Oooh ooh...."

The audience was drop-dead silent. Eve's beautiful voice spiraled into the rafters, sailed across the massive structure like an eagle floating peacefully through the sky. This girl held us in her heart through her powerful voice; and with the words of her final lyrics, "...I could say I love you; but all I can say is.......gee whiz!"

We sprang from our seats in thunderous applause, roaring, screaming, whistling and shouting our pleasure. The Assistant Principal placed his hand on her shoulder, while the audience raved and cried out in passionate approval.

Norman looked at me and just shook his head. He could not believe it, nor could I. Not an ounce of fear was in her voice. It was as if she had been waiting for this day her entire life and she gave her voice to us that day, as a gift.

Where did Eve get this powerful, heavenly voice? She was the talk of the school for days.

We went on to hear and see tap dancers and ballet dancers, and a small jazz band. Now the audience did not know what awaited them, so they were generally courteous. The tap dancers were okay, but with the first ballet dancer, we struggled hard to keep from laughing. She was a lovely girl, tall, with black shiny, long, bouncy hair. She wore a short pink tutu, pink leotards, and black leather ballet shoes. She looked the part, but she was very heavy footed, awkward in fact, and tears were rolling down our faces trying hard not to laugh when she landed, sounding like she was going through the floor. She continued to do pirouettes, glissades and launches across the stage floor. The audience could barely take it. We stifled our laughter so hard; we could have easily gone through the floor with her.

After a jazz band, then a second ballet dancer came to the floor. I had seen this girl before. She had a very distinctive style and walk. Her clothes were not new, not current, but rather a vintage look from the forties, but she wore leg warmers even when it was warm outside. She was slim, taut, and usually alone. Confident in her strides, she carried her own books. Her hair was pulled into a topknot, and it appeared she really did not notice anyone around her, certainly not me.

She stepped to center stage wearing a pink long sleeve leotard, pink matching tights, a pink organza layered tea-length skirt and pink satin ballet pointe shoes.

She walked across the floor in long graceful ballet strides. My eyes were glued to the pink pointes, preceding her. I had watched many ballet practices of my younger sisters, and the older girls wearing pointes, of which there were few, were the most advanced. This girl was in fact a ballerina, and she was fabulous, graceful and soulfully connected to the music. She danced to Puccini's *Madame Butterfly*.

The audience was silent. Our eyes watched this beautiful bronze Black girl, who like a Fire Opal shrouded in pink, sparkled like the gemstone she really was. Her quiet grace stunned us, as we sat amazed at her classical performance.

187

How was it possible these two Black girls, one, intrinsically talented, and the other classically trained, so different in body build - one tiny with a powerful voice and the other probably 5′ 7″ with body elegance that surpassed any student, could send us into such wonder? But that is what we witnessed.

The initially rowdy group of students left the gymnasium in a calm resolve, a lesson for a lifetime would teach us the hushed dignity of talents blossoming, the awakening of sweet life.

I walked with my friends alongside my brother, Norman, and his buddies, realizing that there were so many gifts in this world. I wanted to be opened to receive them. I felt such pride, and even though I could not do those things myself, I enjoyed seeing those talents in others.

As our friends splintered off from us, our home was the last of the group. Norman gently placed his hand on my shoulder. I felt the heat beneath his strong fingers as he shook his head from side to side in disbelief. We smiled and walked the rest of the way in silence.

31

You Can't Go

Norman sat at the dining room table angry. He asked our mother if he could go out with his buddies. She said, "No, you are not going anywhere." He brought home another poor report card, so our mother told him she was having a talk with him later; and repeated he was not going anywhere, and it was a school night.

"You can sulk all you want," our mother said, "but you are not leaving this house."

A number of phone calls came in for Norman. After the few calls I got, Norman looked at me pleadingly to leave the line open. I don't know what was so important; and why 'this panic' to go out and join his friends. It was a school night after all; and it was raining and the temperature dropping steadily, with sleet and snow anticipated. My brother seemed a little better when one of his friends called and said his mother would not let him go either.

I asked Norman if he wanted me to help him with his homework. He shook his head, 'No.' Helping with his homework was something Norman never wanted me to do, even though sometimes he helped me with mine. In fact, he usually said he already did his homework in study hall at school. I was finished with my homework, so I asked Norman if he wanted to play, Chinese checkers. He said, "Okay," in resolve.

In the bottom drawer of the buffet server with the large beveled mirror above it, our family kept all the games and puzzles. We played regular checkers a lot, but I liked the colors of the Chinese checkers metal board painted in bright red, yellow, green, blue, orange and white, with small round punctured holes that kept the marbles from running across the board. The marbles were in the colors of the board, real marbles, not plastic ones.

I picked a color and waited for Norman to select his.

Our mother was sitting in the living room on her favorite Shantung emerald-green upholstered chair, eating her beloved oranges from a plastic grocery store bag. Using a paring knife, she peeled the oranges, in a circular fashion, in an endless pattern from the stem to the navel. Then she dropped the peelings into a trash bag, sliced through the top about an inch from the stem, and gently squeezed until the juice bubbled up to the surface.

The peel was one continuous spiral from beginning to end. When we were younger, we held on to the peeling as my mother cut it with a knife. When she finished, the entire peel fell into our hands, and we marveled at its snake like skin, and the tangy smell of oranges.

***

"I don't think this is fair. Mother is trying to treat me like I'm a baby."

"Norman, if you would do right, maybe she wouldn't have to treat you like that," I said.

"What's the big deal? I'm going to the military when I graduate, anyway. I'm sick of this school business."

"You act like there won't be things in the military you will have to learn. You may have to crack some books there as well."

"At least there, I will get paid. If I get paid, I will do it. Simple!"

"Norman, your incentive is always money. Why can't you do it for yourself?"

Norman didn't respond, but instead said, "Got your man," as he picked up my marble and eyed it with a smile.

"Okay, you got it. It won't take me long to get your man too," I said while eyeing the board.

"Yeah, sure, Beverley. I'll be waiting," he said sarcastically.

It was Norman's night to clean the kitchen, and my night to wash the pots and pans. I let them soak as needed, washed them clean and let them dry on a kitchen towel on the counter. The standard rule was: 'No dirty pots in the sink overnight,' or my father would wake you in the middle of the night, and he didn't care whose turn it was.

Ironically, we were one of the few families with a dish washer in our neighborhood. So, my brothers and I fought over whose turn it was to wash the pots.

It was Orlando's night to sweep the floor and empty the trash in the bin in the alley. Sometimes, Orlando would pay us to do his chores. The chores were rotated between the three of us weekly. My mother usually cooked the dinner, but Orlando got dinner started, until our mother arrived.

Norman and I continued to play Chinese checkers, and eventually he relaxed. He seemed like his old self. The tension from the anger, which made the skin across his smooth face tighten like an elastic band, now gone, leaving the tissue around his eyes soft. He started laughing while we played, and talking silly stuff like, "Bev, didn't you see that. You must be blind!" He definitely had forgotten the emotion which grabbed him earlier.

"Norman," we heard our mother call. He immediately tensed up, switching persona, like a dog awakened from a sleep.

192

Norman raised his head. His chest moved up, then down once, frozen.

My mother called him again. This time, Norman said, "I'm coming."

I looked at him, and he seemed angry again. Leaving the table, not like a boy, but a man, who didn't want anyone messing with his life.

Picking up the pieces of the Chinese checkers, I slid the marbles into individual clear plastic bags by color, then placed the bags inside the round metal container. My mother and brother were still talking in the living room. I mean my mother was talking, and Norman just stood there, motionless and speechless, as I passed them going up the stairs, holding the banister of the white painted spindles of the stairway.

The next morning, the phone ringing about 6:00 a.m. awakened me. I heard my mother call for my brother Norman to come to her room. I got up quietly, in my pink flannel nightgown, and followed him to the door. My father was still asleep as my mother handed Norman the phone. I heard Norman say, "No man, it's not true. It's not true," as he crumbled to the floor, my mother grabbed him before he fell.

"What's wrong?" I asked anxiously, my heart pounding in my chest, watching Norman in slow motion - slump down to the thin wall to wall carpeting like a discarded teddy bear, sobbing.

I looked to my mother for answers. Her eyes were red, face puffy with indentations from her pillow and hands perhaps, and tears were rolling gently down her face.

My mother rose from the floor. Norman was still lying there, crying softly. "There was a car accident last night," she whispered and took a deep breath. "One of your brother's friends was killed and two are in the emergency room with broken bones and bruises."

"What?" I asked, frightened for which friend it could possibly be. I knew all four of his friends in the car that evening. Each, like Norman, was a year older than me.

My mother said an incident was reported on the 11:00 p.m. news last night. She heard the broadcast, but had not made the connection to Norman's friends, as she waited to watch her favorite show, *Late Night with Johnny Carson*.

Norman stood up and wiped the tears which blanketed his face with the back of his hand. Our father was awoken, startled, he asked, "What's this? What's going on?"

Our mother said immediately, "Don't worry, Norm. Go back to sleep. You need your rest for work. I'll take the children downstairs." She ushered us out of their bedroom, and we went downstairs to the dining room. The second phone was located there on a phone bench table with a padded seat, very popular during the fifties and sixties.

It didn't bother me that our father was too sleepy to get involved in issues of his children. The truth was that he didn't like any of our friends anyway. Their families did not rise to the standards he expected. He always thought he was better than all of us.

My mother went into the kitchen and made breakfast.

"Who was it, Norman?" I probed when we were alone. "Who died?"

A blank look crossed Norman's face, as if momentarily there was no recollection of a death, as he lifted his eyes and lowered them. Then a single tear trickled down his soft face, passing the outer edge of his nostril, disappearing into the corner of his mouth. He lowered his head. "It was Nathaniel." My heart sank to the pit of my stomach.

'God,' I said to myself. 'How could it be Nathaniel?'

He was one of the nicest guys at school, always courteous, with the most beautiful voice. He sang many solos with the school choir. Our school was noted for its music preparation, with many students auditioning and selected for the Indianapolis All City and the Indiana All State choirs, string ensembles, orchestras, madrigals and jazz and band competitions. Nathaniel was so handsome with dark brown thick eyebrows with every strand in place and curly lashes that looked like they had been individually placed with glue, easily suggesting he had a weekly appointment at Max Factor. He had dark brown eyes and sun-kissed natural copper skin.

That classic 50's style was Nathaniel's look, with hair neatly cut with a fade on the side. He often wore double breasted suits to school with padded shoulders, and suspenders clipped to his pleated front trousers just barely touching the tip of his shiny leather shoes. His oxford shirt collar was always opened, and it was rare to see him in a tie, except for very special occasions. Needless to say, he was far better dressed than the other male students at school.

I felt like the air was knocked out of me. My chest heaved up and down, as I battled to breathe. 'Why Nathaniel? Why him?' I couldn't understand it. He was a wonderful, good, kind, and generous person. Then, a voice in my head whispered, 'The good die young.' I heard this expression many times, and it seemed true. 'Yes, the good die young,' I repeated the adage to myself, as my heart hustled, beating faster.

Poor Norman! I felt so badly for him. Nathaniel was such a good friend and role model, and ironically, unlike Norman's other friends, Nathaniel was an honor student. Although his other friends were mentally sharp, they were not interested in school. Nathaniel never cut class, nor did he criticize Norman and his other buddies who did.

He was mature for his age. I was always proud of him and proud to be around him. He made you feel special; but the truth was, he was the one who was special. And his sphere of influence and kindness just pulled you into his circumference. He was clearly remarkable, always setting the appropriate example. Norman truly admired him.

Sometimes, I saw Nathaniel in the hallway wearing his honor badge, which was given to students on the Honor Roll. The badge, with your name imprinted on it, gave you the privilege of leaving class early. I felt like the two of us were in a special club, along with other classmates who also wore the sacred badge. He stopped by to say hello from time to time, while I was on hall duty, checking passes and making sure other students were only going where their passes indicated they could go.

I would never say that someone else, even me, should have left this world instead of Nathaniel. God alone determines that; but he had so much to offer. In his sixteen-year life, he had done more good in this world, than other people three times his age.

Norman's other buddies survived, and we were all grateful. My brother could never have emotionally survived the loss of all his friends. He did nothing alone, always with his friends, even his Burger Chef job. A couple of his friends worked there too.

That day, Norman did not go to school. His friends, classmates, and neighbors called to talk to him. I saw some of his classmates at school, many rushing to ask how Norman was, and expressed surprise he had not been with them. Even Norman's teachers asked about him. Everyone was devastated about Nathaniel. The principal extended a moment of silence over the public address system for Nathaniel and the speedy recovery of the other boys.

The boy driving, small frame, had no injuries, only a few bruises. I saw him at school and was surprised to see him. He looked like he had died with Nathaniel. My heart went out to him. When he saw me, he came up and asked, "Norman Okay? ...I don't know what happened; but I know it's my fault.... I'll come by and see Norman tomorrow." Other guys came up to him, providing a safe passage. With the popularity of Nathaniel, who knows what could happen. The students, however, were very kind to him, and he needed their comfort and understanding to get through this difficult time.

When my mother got home from work, we went to the hospital to visit the other boys, who were faring well. Thankfully! They would probably be released soon. There was talk of concern regarding head injury, and the doctors wanted to monitor their progress. They were so happy to see Norman and told him they were glad he was not with them.

My mother and I extended greetings to their families. My mother gave the boys hugs, careful not to hold tight. They had lots of dark bruises over their bodies. But these boys had come to our house all the time. If not in the house, they were in the alley, playing ball.

The next Saturday afternoon, Norman's friend, the driver of the fatal crash, came by the house. He stood at the front door, his head lowered in homage and pain. His left hand bandaged and dark bruises were on the right side of his pale face. Norman looked, said nothing, then, opened the door.

As Norman opened the door, his buddy said, "I'm sorry man," with a sadness permeating every inch of his demeanor.

Norman grabbed him and for a moment, both boys, locked in pain, cried.

Tears flooded my face too. I wondered how they would get through all this.

"I know you loved him man," Norman said. "It was an accident."

"But I killed Nathaniel," his friend said through blubbering tears. "It was all my fault. I can't fix this!"

It was an accident, Norman repeated. "You have a good heart, man. It was an accident, you gotta' remember that."

I was proud of my brother for trying to console his friend. Norman seemed grown up and not the little boy who was always running around having a good time. Yet I was crushed, feeling a tightness across my neck and shoulders.

The boys would have a lifetime to reconcile the loss of their friend. My brother, with his arms around his friend's shoulder, lumbered with him down the sidewalk to a vehicle waiting. I could not tell who was driving. A cousin, I think.

Later, my brother's other friend, the one whose mother said he couldn't go either, came to the house. He was driving his mother's large baby blue Pontiac Bonneville, with sparkling chrome and large headlights screaming in the sun, with baby blue interior. Definitely custom! He was picking up their other friends who had been released by the hospital at their homes. I asked Norman if I could come along? He looked at his buddy and they both said, "Sure." From the look on her face, my mother felt better knowing I was going. I sat on the large padded leather front passenger seat and listened as the details of the car crash unfolded.

From what they could put together, along with witness accounts and the Highway Patrol report, the two injured boys, (now in the car with us) were riding in the backseats laughing, singing and talking at the time of the accident. The radio was blasting rock n' roll tunes. The guys remembered singing, "Good Vibration" and the Beatles, "I Want to Hold Your Hands." The driver was talking with Nathaniel who was seated in the passenger seat; while trying to listen to their conversation from the back and singing, when traffic on Hwy 421 two-lane highway started backing up.

"Man, he was worried about us being late…. We told him it didn't matter; cause we were just having fun anyway."

But anticipating being late and losing patience, their friend thought he could pass the cars in front of him, by overtaking them with speed, thinking he had sufficient time to cross over into on-coming traffic and return to his lane. What he had not anticipated was the sleet turning to ice, black ice, on the overpass above White River.

"Man," the boys said, "It happened so fast. Next thing we knew, we were flying across the interstate hitting everything in our way. When the car stopped, we realized for the first time Nathaniel was not with us…. These broken bones don't even compare to what happened to him, and the terror we felt at that moment."

My stomach fell to the floor, as I crossed my arms and pulled them tightly against my chest, my fist in tight balls. I learned Nathaniel had been thrown from the wreckage.

***

School went on as before. It seemed like the last year didn't really happen. In my mind, I could see Nathaniel laughing and joking in the hallways, but he was gone. My brothers and his friends started to take life more seriously. They rarely cut school anymore, had better passing grades, and prepared for commencement.

A couple of the boys got part-time jobs after school, working at Burger Chef, which Norman seemed to like. Some nights he would bring home several hamburgers that didn't sell and the manager allowed the boys to take. Norman, Eddie and I ate them at the dining room table.

At graduation, I stood in line next to Norman. It was a beautiful June evening. I was wearing a new powder blue dress with a white collar beneath my robe, and Norman a new suit. He accumulated enough credits to participate. In line, his friends popped over to talk and laugh with Norman. The guys looked happy, with no mention of Nathaniel.

A couple of the guys were enlisting in the armed services and the others were going to work for RCA. Norman was anxious to go to the Navy. I had misgivings about that decision due to the war in Vietnam. What if he didn't make it back? I was afraid for him and would miss him.

202

Our father was not at our graduation, and we didn't expect to see him anyway. He had to work or wanted to work. My father frankly thought that these commemorative activities were a waste of time. The only graduation he attended for me was my graduation from college. Our mother and siblings attended our celebrations with smiles plastered across their faces.

32

Black Boy Standing

My father never saw himself as a black man in America. He saw himself as a Jamaican. He thought Black men in America were basically lazy. Yet, all the Black men living on our street had good jobs. One was on the commission for the fire department, one drove a city bus and was formerly a soldier in the Korean War. Another was a dentist with his own practice on the next block and he drove a custom pink Cadillac, and generally the other men worked for RCA, Chrysler Corporation, Ford Motor Company and General Motors. They were not lazy at all. My father did not believe in the racial/ethnic premise that Dr. Martin Luther King Jr. sought after and died for. In fact, he criticized him for being non-violent, for expecting Black people to follow him. I'm sure he thought that he would have made the better role model.

But growing up in Jim Crow Indianapolis, I began to see how Black men and Black people in general were pigeonholed in a society that did not want to include them. Statistics say one in every three Black male, babies born would be incarcerated. Black men were eight times more likely to be killed by police than white men.

It was my junior year of high school, and my period three class, which I spent as a service worker for the Dean of Women, a coveted position I'd earn by being an honor roll student and having good behavior. This time just before the first lunch, when rarely anyone was sent out of class for misbehavior, I spent doing homework or research work for my classes, as well as sorting slips for students sent out of class for misbehavior. There was a mahogany Mormon style table desk with a straight-back chair, just before the door leading to the Dean's inner office.

I sat at this table each day, quietly content. Magnificent leaded glass windows let in a profusion of sunlight, with a wide view of the street with shops and apartment buildings, reminding me of a Charles Dickens novel. During school hours, very few people were seen on the street, other than an occasional car waiting to pick up a student.

This day, when I looked out, I saw my brother Norman standing across the street, like he was waiting for someone. I thought he was having some girlfriend problem, because the night before, he was on the phone late into the night talking to his girlfriend. He looked lonely out there. Then I started feeling apprehensive, and my breathing took on a conscious level of concern. This is Jim Crow Indianapolis. A Black boy could not stand on the street without drawing suspicion. It was not likely that a truant officer would be interested, because he was directly across the street from the school. If he really wanted to cut school, he would have gone further.

What was my brother doing out there? He is a Black boy. It wasn't safe for him out there, even in broad daylight. I watched him standing there. I was afraid to even acknowledge that he was my brother, because of this class. But at least this class gave me the latitude to run to the phone booth, to call my mother for help. I never would have called my father.

He was an easy target. Just what was he thinking? Then, two police cars pulled up quietly, no sirens, and the officers got out. They started talking to my brother. I could not hear what was said.

My heart felt like I had just finished running a race. I stood up, looked into the Dean's office. She was working on papers. I asked if I could have the hall pass to go to the restroom. She said, "Yes, of course," not even looking up from her desk. I walked quietly out of the office, then dashed to the 1930's phone booth at the end of the hall. I called my mother at work. She arrived momentarily. Her job was probably ten minutes from the school off of highway 421.

Back in the Dean's office, I was quiet, never mentioning the incident involving my brother to the Dean. Many female students wanted to work in this office, and I did not want to jeopardize my position. Granted, I would not be moved immediately, but I may not get the opportunity the next semester.

I went on to lunch and two other classes, before it was time for my mother to pick me up from school. When she did, my mother told me my brother had been apprehended for burglary and taken to Juvenile Hall. Exasperated, I repeated, "For burglary! Norman would never steal a thing."

My mother continued saying the store Norman was standing in front of was burglarized. The owner called the police. He didn't know when it happened, either that morning or the night before, but Norman was the only person standing out front, so they assumed he did it and he was waiting for a get-away car to take him from the crime scene.

My mother contacted her boss to see if he could help. He left work as well and joined her, but to no avail. They told her boss my brother would not be released, and they were incarcerating him in juvenile detention. Our mother was totally destroyed. She did not even tell my father, because he would be so angry Norman was cutting school. He would feel Norman got just what he deserved.

Norman stayed in detention for one week. My father didn't know, because he worked day and nights. When he came home from his second job around 1:00 a.m., we were all asleep. With the help of our mother's boss, who had a son of his own and was a psychiatrist with many resources, my brother was finally released, and all charges were dropped.

The following year after graduation, Norman joined the Navy, then worked as a paramedic and later became a police officer for the same division which recognized him as, "The Black boy standing." He committed one act of aggression, "Standing while Black," God forbid, on a public street in Indiana.

33

Chuck

In high school, Chuck was a lot of fun. Medium height, but much taller than me and slim, he always made me laugh with his wonderful sense of humor. Chuck was Norman's friend and classmate. In spite of all the joy, he brought to our lives, he had to channel the pain in his own life.

Chuck's father, a social studies teacher, was one of the first artificial heart transplant patients in Indianapolis, Indiana. Had it not been for Chuck, I probably would not have known anything about this advancement in medical science. The procedure, as I understood at the time, was a temporary method for those awaiting an actual heart transplant.

I remember watching television with my mother and siblings when a man, Chuck's father I believed, was being interviewed with the drowning sound of machine pumping blood through his veins and arteries. As the interviewer asked questions about this new way of living, I became really quiet. The sound emanating from the machine was overwhelming, and I noticed my heart and breathing began to imitate the rhythm and tempo of the equipment. Fortunately, his father was able to talk and share.

I wondered how he slept with all that external noise dominating every inch of space in his hospital room. In my mind, he had to be sedated to sleep. That monster contraption was alarming to me. It had hoses and wires extending from every direction, and barely left enough room for the patient to sit in a chair or walk from one side of the bed to the other.

Chuck was hoping his father would survive the initial artificial heart and then later be a patient for the actual heart transplant. He seemed to know everything about the procedure.

This was incredible to me. First, to think you could live on an artificial heart for any length of time and then to have an actual human heart transplanted in your chest. This was scary as well as painful I thought.

But Chuck had a real positive attitude. He believed that even if his father didn't survive the artificial heart, he would significantly contribute to the science of mankind and for that, Chuck was so proud.

I was afraid for his father and I know Chuck was too, but he was brave, like his father. He worried about his own health, because this was a genetic disorder. Chuck hoped he wouldn't succumb to the same health issues. Therefore, he always stayed active: played basketball, ran track, jogged on his own time and always watched what he ate.

***

Chuck's father did not survive his artificial heart. However, he lived a number of years with it, a truly remarkable achievement indeed.

***

More than twenty-five years later, Chuck went to a super-bowl game, excited and cheerful. As his buddies waited for him in the lobby, Chuck succumbed to a massive heart attack. In spite of his daily runs, more than five to seven miles a day, good diet, body mass within normal limits, Chuck could not survive the genetics of his life.

34

Music Camp

Each summer I looked forward to music camp. I spent a week there with students from all over Indiana, wanting to hone our skills in preparation for the spring state competition; and who knows, we might even get a music scholarship to college. The camp was not free, my father paid for my registration and stay.

Once we arrived and got off the buses with luggage, we were assigned cabins, mates and latrines. There were fifteen to twenty students assigned to each cabin; and most often than not, I was the only child of color in my cabin; but generally, there were seven to ten Negro students at the camp of approximately 250 music lovers. One girl Carol, I knew from my neighborhood. Our mothers shared the rides for us to numerous music rehearsals and concerts. Many times, on Saturday mornings, we walked in the Indiana cold to the school where the rehearsal was taking place or in the heat during the summer. Ironically, walking in the cold felt like sitting in the back seat of Carol's mother's van. They loved driving with the windows open in the dead of winter. I, on the other hand, froze my little skinny butt off in my wool coat, camel colored French tam, and fake cashmere neck scarf.

Carol and I were good buddies. She was taller and bigger than me, (but many kids were), and very kind. On those walks, we shared confidences such as our fears, student body elections, boyfriends, music competitions, etc. Carol played the bass violin and I, the viola. Her mother picked up her instrument at school on Fridays, which allowed Carol to walk home with her friends.

***

The campsite was really a lovely and peaceful environment, with magnificent trees, like black maple, ash, oak, black walnuts, and fir trees as well. The trees formed a bridge of comfort, providing shade as the sun shifted its light, or buffered us from the wind playfully blowing leaves across the ground. The massive grass fields and landings were freshly cut just before our arrival using the large, motorized riding mower I saw in the old red barn. The smell of freshly cut grass penetrated our nostrils; but it was a good scent, a lovely summer smell.

Every morning after wash-up at the latrine, (it was difficult for me to tolerate the ice-cold showers), we lined up and proceeded to our assigned tables in the mess hall. After our blessing, led by a Chaplin, we were served oatmeal (which I did not like), French toast on one day and a couple of days - bacon or a sausage patty was served. I was surprised how fast the kids ate their oatmeal. I was used to Jamaican cornmeal porridge in the winter months or cream of wheat, but never oatmeal at home. Once or twice during the week, we had scrambled eggs. Every day, milk, juice and water, as well as toast with butter was available, so there was always something you could eat, and something you were familiar with.

By 8:30 a.m., we were off to the latrine again, then back to the cabins to get our instruments and music, before heading to our first class, which began promptly at 9:00. At 12:00 noon, lunch was served in the mess hall. From 1:00 to 3:00, the orchestra rehearsal took place, followed by playtime or rest time till 6:00 p.m. During this period, you could read, hang out with friends, swim in the pool or lake, play tennis, practice or sleep. Sometimes, I worked with the newspaper group, helping with the drawings for our weekend newsletter. Dinner was served at 6:00 p.m., followed by sectional rehearsals at 7:30 to 8:30 p.m. Lights were out at 10:00 p.m., although we stayed up late and talked about everything until we were lifeless, and then the activities started again the next day.

The Friday night before we would leave on Sunday, we had a big camp out, where we sat on logs placed in a horseshoe shape around a huge campfire. We sang songs, told jokes, ate S'mores and shared stories. Sunday afternoons when our parents came to pick us up, we performed a symphony concert, a band concert, and a string orchestra program, as a culmination of our work. After the program, cookies and punch were served, and a small student jazz band entertained during the reception.

214

I was so glad to see my family, and they were happy to see me too. Orlando and Norman carried my instrument and luggage to the car. Everyone waited as the campers said final 'goodbyes,' through smiles and tears.

Every year music camp filled my life with hope. I was different from most of my friends and family, because I was part of a music dominion which no one I knew from home or the neighborhood, except Carol, was part of. I developed into the person I wanted to be, and was respected, supported and loved by my friends and family.

***

During my last summer of music camp, the first couple of days went well, with beautiful sunsets over the lake I witnessed in an aperture of light through the trees. I was drawn into marvelous shades of Mandarin orange blending into blood reds and purples. Magnificent! The dazzling sunrise that morning was yet another reminder of nature's power to overwhelm me. The weather was slightly cool. It was uncomfortable as we headed over for breakfast at 7 a.m. I wore a sweater with my freezing hands digging deep into my pockets. Not even the addition of a cotton undershirt helped much. My chest twitched back and forth from the cold. By noon, the sky was a blackened purple and by two o'clock a wind started a blustering approach. We knew the signs.

After the close of our 3:00 class, the storm broke. We ran clumsily carrying instruments, with paper and jackets covering our heads. We were plummeted by raindrops, the size of cherry tomatoes. Before we got back to our rooms, hail pelted us, stinging our arms and legs with BB gun-like pellets. Soaked and wet, my body tingled. The umbrella was no use in the strong wind. We were happy to get away from nature's fury.

In the cabin, heat and humidity greeted us. The smell of wet clothing and soaked shoes permeated the air, as we quickly removed our wet garments.

I jumped into my bunk, the other girls did as well, and covered up. The cabin, although humid, was quiet. Only the sound of thunder in the distance and rain and hail pelting the roof was heard. The sky darkened. No light penetrated the metal framed glass windows, perfect for sleeping. Before I knew it, I had drifted off. The wrangler bell for dinner rang ten minutes before six. We got up, readied, and hauled our butts over to the mess hall feeling quite sluggish. There was, however, something quite chilling about the temperature in the room, even though the rain outside was light now and the winds had subsided.

The campers stood, as was customary, and sang our blessing that evening, *Praise God from whom all blessings flow. Praise him all creatures here below. Praise him above the heavenly host. Praise Father, Son and Holy Ghost.* When we sat down, the director told us that one of our camp counselors was killed late that afternoon in the storm. He was trying to re-connect the boats to the dock, when he was struck by one of the sails, knocked in the water, unconscious, and before another staffer could get to him, he drowned.

You could hear quiet escapes of breaths, moans of "Oh No" as a hush took over the room. There were barely audible sobs, heavy breathing, and I saw tears run down the faces of kids at our tables. I was stunned. He was our age, 17 or 18 years old.

While we were busy each day over the last four years with our music, this young man was helping to make camp a better place. I saw him at our meals, serving us, taking dishes and utensils back, sweeping the tennis courts where leaves were blown in, and tying boats to the slip on the small marina. And as is sometimes awkward between boys and girls, I never asked his name, and I did not know the protocol between campers and workers of the same age; and he was white and I, Black. He was a nice-looking young man with sandy hair, slim, but strong, wearing t-shirts and rough-dried Bermuda shorts. He was always pleasant and smiled. As we scurried to classes, I saw him talking to guys mostly at the camp, only a couple of girls did he seemed to know. Again, I wonder why 'the good die young?' 'What a beautiful life he could have had, but it was never promised.'

The food was brought out to the tables, but many plates were left untouched, particularly by girls who knew him. I went ahead and ate along with a few other girls and boys at my table, but I knew the others could barely get a swallow down between tears. I suppose it was expedient to tell us this news at the same time; but I thought it might have been better to have the camp counselors share this sad message in our cabins, where individual grief would not be viewed among 250 campers.

***

The next day was beautiful. Cumulous nimbus clouds moved smoothly about the blue sky, following me as I headed to pay my respects to the young man, at the same location I last saw him. The marina was clear, as I heard sails flapping in the wind. The water closest to the lakeshore was a sea green and it advanced into shades of indigo blues the further out you looked. I blinked my eyes, trying to sharpen my focus as the boats, just a few and mostly canoes, rocked up and down, back and forth with the rhythm of the water hitting the shoreline.

The lake looked so peaceful, and the warm wind just barely slapped my sleeveless arms, as I detected a faint fishy smell. How could this lovely place have taken the last breath of his life, and then moved on as if nothing had happened. How was this possible? As I turned to leave, I saw others coming to pay their last respects. They wanted to see as well, to pay their last respect. They wanted to reconcile the new day with the sad events of the afternoon before, where one of us (and it could have been anyone of us) was taken out, swiftly and immediately. This young man's memory was now a part of the landscape.

218

***

In my senior year, I applied to a couple of colleges in Indiana for a music scholarship. I was please to get an offer from various schools, and selected Ball State University, because my neighbor Sandy attended school there. The scholarship paid my tuition for four years, but my family still had to pay for my room and board, and books.

My father told me he would pay for my first year. I was happy about that, but he said, "That's it!" I didn't understand how that could be it; but my second year, just as he said, 'That was really it.' He refused to pay another penny. I was his only child in college, Orlando working fulltime with a family, and Norman in the Navy, stationed in Vietnam on a carrier. No money was coming from my father.

Before my sophomore year, I went to the financial aid office, like other students, only to be rejected. They said my father made too much money, and therefore I did not qualify for financial aid. I pleaded with the officer, trying to assure him I could not make my father pay for my expenses, when he flatly refused. And what was truly irritating was the fact my father still claimed me as one of his dependents for taxes. Even though I had financial problems, my mother kept me dressed in the best that L.S. Ayres, William H. Block and Levi Strauss department stores had to offer (as long as the apparel was on sale or part of the Pre-Fall sale).

I also earned money working in the music library five days a week in the semesters. My father got me a summer job each year as a cashier in the gas company. They provided a summer job program for children of employees who were enrolled in college. One advantage for the company, was the use of students to fill vacancies of their staff members on summer vacations.

Each year I went before a committee to convince them of my need for financial aid. Finally, in my junior year, the committee shared that the Federal Government expanded the National Defense Education/Authorization loan under President Lyndon Johnson to include struggling poor inner cities throughout the United States. With this loan for students in the field of education, the loan had to be paid back in the following ways: New teachers were needed to teach in inner city schools; and if you did so, the loan would be paid back until the full obligation was met. This worked for me. I must add that my father paid for years of private lessons for me and my brothers and sisters at Jordan College Conservatory of Music, because he wanted us to play in his future church. However, he would not pay when it did not benefit him. This was only important to me.

***

When I think back on my summer music camp experience, I am grateful. Music camp encouraged and supported my preparation whereby I could confidently participate with other students, placing first and or second in State music competitions playing the viola. It also brought to my life an understanding and appreciation for my life pursuit of music, which started as a music teacher at age twenty-one. I will remember for all of my life, the young man who was among those who made my experience at the camp enjoyable and comfortable, even though his own dreams were not fulfilled.

35

The Movie

In 1987, Norman called me on the telephone to tell me he was premiering in a movie, filmed in Indiana about the tragedy of narcotics and the 'War on Drugs' as President Nixon coined this phrase nearly two decades before. He was so excited, and I was happy for him. My siblings went to see his performance on the big screen. He played the role of a bad guy. Having spent many years as a detective in both the narcotics and homicide divisions, he understood all the roles very clearly. The film industry wanted someone who could immediately absorb that life, so a police officer was chosen. Later, Norman also served in another precarious role, investigating cops who had gone rogue.

During this time, major community resources around the world, were spent on trying to infiltrate this mega industry, and it still is today. The U.S. Dept. of Justice states that most of the people arrested for drug involvement in the United States were Black. The New England Journal of Medicine reported that of the increasing numbers of incarcerated drug offenders, 27% are Black, 7% Hispanic and 15% are white. It was clear that white people, who have the money, power, access, connections and resources, were significant players, but were not substantially represented in the prison population.

The movie identified the corrupt players working behind the scenes, such as city government representatives, corporate businessmen, and heads of police departments.

Norman knew this domain well. He understood all the players. On a regular basis he witnessed the ugliness, the innocence of young people pulled into this life, the deaths and the devastation of families. He was not afraid. My brother, who was afraid of his own shadow as a child, became a confident, self-assured man.

One day Norman told me about the death of one of our high school friends, Darryl, who was new on the narcotics team. They were on the police force together. Darryl had been working as an undercover officer, but did not know that his cover had been blown. As he approached the suspect's front door and rang the bell, the suspect shot through the door. He died instantly, sending the narcotics officers into major realignment. A deployment of officers were drawn into a gun battle in a residential neighborhood.

Norman was a pallbearer at Darryl's service. I imagined a procession of officers in cars from all over the state, quietly following the funeral hearse in mass respect with their vehicle lights on. I was living in California and could not afford to attend.

I knew Darryl pretty well in high school and had gone on a couple of dates with him to the pizza parlor and to the Dairy Queen for ice cream on a Sunday afternoon. Darryl always drove a nice car. I assumed it belonged to his parents, but never asked. He was very nice, and was always a gentleman. He and I were just not meant to be. I dated other boys and went to college. He attended the police academy after high school and later married. I was happy for him. However, his first child died of Sudden Infant Death Syndrome. I was crushed by that knowledge. Good police officers are heroes. The lives of police officers are difficult, They courageously and selflessly sign up to protect and serve, regardless of the personal risks they take or the challenges they confront in their professional and private lives.

Yes, Norman knew the professional side: honor, duty, obligations, and law. He also knew the corrosive side: silence, loyalty, fear and control. Both sides chose the gun as their weapon of choice, whether it was issued to you, stolen by you, or given to you. Both sides valued money above all. It was always about money, so you could pay workers, build your dynasty, and give your family a better life, while staying undetected with your armies of soldiers (one on the right side of the law, and the other on the wrong side). The residue of addiction and its impact on families and communities was overwhelming. Opioids have caused the same problem today, but it is not a 'War on Drugs.' Although in general, addiction is now considered a disease, but generally Black people are still treated as criminals. This is what the movie tried to depict – how tough life was on both sides.

36

Fiftieth

Years passed and I became a mother, a school administrator, and support my family and friends. Civil Rights laws were prominent, yet there were still many negative impacts in communities and cities. Black men still had to be proactive and protective of their environment. The United States of America was still reacting from trouble within with white nationalist organization demanding things remain the same. The struggle with women's rights as well as foreign entities leaving deeply rooted scares on our nation with the aftermath of 9-11 in New York.

My brothers, however, were still with me, active and present in my life.

***

In 1997, Orlando came from Indiana to visit me in California for my fiftieth birthday, 1997. My brother Eddie accompanied him and paid for his ticket. With his doctor's permission, Orlando boarded the plane. He looked forward to visiting Los Angeles and spending some time in the desert as well.

My older brother had been ill for a number of years being a victim after a drag racing incident in his twenties. He was in the hospital for almost a year with a myriad of injuries. He suffered an enlarge heart from the trauma of that incident.

Orlando said he had something very special for me and he wanted to give me his gift in person.

***

It had been one year since I last saw Orlando, when I visited all my siblings in Indiana. During that visit, I had a rude awakening about healthcare issues in America.   When Clarence and I went to see him, he didn't look well at all, even though he tried to entertain us with his enthusiasm about his fish in various aquariums, particularly the predatory ones. Two of the tanks were about 150 gallons each. He always loved fish, and as a boy, Orlando had fish in small tanks that he took good care of. Here in his duplex which he owned with my father, he took pride in his huge aquariums and the smaller feeder tanks he used to sustain the larger fish. Orlando was fascinated by his aquatic animals.

But there was a look in his eyes that spoke directly to his illness. It was clear to me.

I asked him if he had taken his medicine. He said, "No."

"Why not?" I retorted angrily.

He straightened up, no longer bending over the fish tank. Something in him changed, and he was no longer the 'happy go lucky' guy telling jokes, that I knew well. He lowered his head, then said like he was stating a simple fact, "Because, I can't afford it."

"What do you mean, 'You can't afford it?'" I shot back like I was *his* big sister.

With his head still down, he softly replied, "Because, I can't, Bev."

"Well, give me your prescriptions and Clarence and I will go to the pharmacy and fill it," I said. I was so angry with him. How could he begin to get well if he did not take his medicine as prescribed?

Orlando gave me his prescriptions and directions to the Rexall drugstore nearby.

We dashed off. Clarence waited in the car while I went in and placed Orlando's prescription.

When I returned to the car, medicine in hand, I slumped down into the seat and cried. "How can they do this to him?"

Clarence responded immediately, "What's wrong, Beverley? Why are you crying? Do what?" He reached over and put his arms around my shoulders.

"What's wrong?" he repeated.

I grabbed Kleenex from my purse, blew my nose, and then said just above a whisper, "Orlando's medicines cost over

$750.00. How could they do that to him?" I turned my head slowly from side to side. "One heart medication was five hundred dollars for only a month supply of pills. Do you hear me? How can they do that to people?" My voice got louder. "This is 1996!"

My heart sank to my stomach, knowing I could never buy his medicine again. I used my credit card to pay. My brother's medicines were a death sentence. I was shocked and I was hurt!

***

When my brothers arrived at my home, Orlando was so excited to give me his gift. I sat down in the breakfast room and carefully opened the box. It was a porcelain Black doll. I removed the doll from its wrapping and tissues, and then placed the doll on the metal stand I pulled from the box. The doll was uniquely beautiful. I stared at her, and then turned to my brother, who was watching me intensely, and smiled.

My eyes immediately focused on the navy blue and white floral print dress the doll wore with traces of white light creeping through branches of the trees. It was a handmade garment a child in Jamaica would wear, with a gathered elastic band pulled down across her shoulder. An overhang of the same fabric extended around the bodice and empire waist. The doll was barefooted, like so many children in the West Indies. When I saw the doll's feet, I thought of the story my mother told me.

***

As a child, I walked late. My mother said that she didn't realize that I did not like my bare feet to touch the ground. One day, she bought me a pair of red shoes to go with my Easter outfit. When she put the shoes on, I stood up and walked confidently about, as she expected me to do months before. I still don't like to walk barefoot.

***

Interestingly, the doll's fingers were raised in a demure fashion, with wrists accented by gold bangles, like the ones I wore most of my life. The doll also wore an ankle bracelet, another accessory common to the island. I imagined my brother probably did a drawing of what he wanted, because the doll's head was lowered and cast shyly to the side.

Orlando said the doll reminded him of me when I was a child. He said I was quiet and shy. I distinctly remember being quiet, but shy would never have crossed my mind. But I recalled how artistically talented my brother was. He could draw well, received awards for his talent at school. I imagined he first did the drawing, with all the details he could muster, and gave it to a doll maker. He said the doll maker was a friend of his. It was a stunning replica.

***

229

Today, the doll still stands on a table in my bedroom. Her curly black hair with a white ribbon on top, reminds me daily of the little girl my big brother knew, 50 years earlier.

37

Enough Time

I thought I had enough time. I worked out everything in my head. I talked with Orlando. He was in the hospital in Indiana. I told him that as soon as I got the word from Clarence's doctor that he was okay, I would be there to help him. Clarence was having cancer surgery and I had to be there to support him. Orlando was his usual kind self when I talked to him the day before.

"Don't worry Beverley. You have to be there for your husband. I understand that. I'll be here, when you can get here. Don't worry about me."

But I was worried. He was divorced many years now with no children nearby to help him. His grown children were raising their own families now. So yes, life gets complicated. He had a girlfriend who cooked for him. But it was not the same as having family to help.

I was really torn emotionally. Orlando was always there for me, whenever I needed him. I had apologized to him often over the years after he asked me to raise his daughter Jean. Clarence and I willingly accepted. However, I never anticipated his daughter would think of her Uncle Clarence more as her father figure than her own father. I was pained by this; but Orlando took this in stride as well.

"All I want is for her to be cared for and loved in a good family," Orlando said. He was so selfless, I thought.

I continued with tears in my eyes, "But Orlando, she doesn't think of you as her father."

"That doesn't matter to me. I just wanted one of my children to have a life I could not provide them. Really Bev, I can live with that. I just want her to be in a good family."

I was bothered by it. My brother willingly gave up fatherhood, to provide his child a better life. I felt that regardless of the life he could provide, his child was better off with him.

***

I was ready to support my husband and my thinking was that within a week or so, I would leave for Indiana to help Orlando. I made arrangements with family and friends to help Clarence.

The morning of Clarence's surgery, I was waiting in the pre-op surgery room, when I received a call from my sister. I stepped into the wide corridor for privacy, where sunshine blanketed me from the large plate glass windows. I leaned against the window ledge, probably twelve inches deep, when I heard my sister's voice say, "Bev, I just talked with the nurse. Orlando died this morning. He didn't make it."

"No, no! I didn't get there to help him," I said as my stomach knotted in pain.

I placed my hand against the window, still cool, in spite of the intensive sunlight coming in. My grief overwhelmed me. My face saturated with tears. I felt like I would collapse. A nurse advancing towards me for her early morning shift asked if she could help. I saw her faintly through my blurred vision, as I straightened. She handed me Kleenex, which I took.

"Are you sure you're all right?" she asked.

I gestured I was going to the pre-op room. I'm sure she thought my state was related to why I was there.

I wiped my eyes and said, "Thank you." When I lifted my hands, I realized the phone was still in my hand. I put the phone to my ear, and I could hear my sister's voice again.

"Beverley, are you okay?"

"Yes," I said, still wiping tears running profusely down my face; but I knew it wasn't entirely true. I would never be truly okay again. My big brother was gone. The one who I held on to when I first arrived in America, the one who walked me to school, the one who started our weekday dinners, the one who fixed our cars, the one who drove me to and from college and never complained, and the one who was always proud of me.

***

Years later, Clarence and I were driving in rush hour traffic in Beverly Hills after leaving a shopping center. Redirected by traffic officers because of congestion, we ended up lost. I could not understand how we could be lost when we were only about ten minutes from the shopping center we just left. But each turn we made, sent us into a rash of redirection – can't turn left here or right there. We were totally frustrated. When we made the last turn, I looked up to see the street name. Orlando's name was right in front of me on the sign. The street was Orlando Avenue. After seeing my brother's name before me in bold letters, something calming came over me. I was immediately soothed. Orlando was with me. I had nothing to worry about.

38

Hold On!

My older brothers brought a lot of joy to my life, and certainly brought intrigue and excitement. Between 1951 and 1956, three more siblings were born into our family here in America, and I did my part in helping to rear them as children, when our mother worked. But as adults, we had a wonderful time sharing the joys and supporting the sorrows in our lives. Every moment with all my brothers and sisters held the possibility of enlightenment, surprise, challenges and wonder. I reflect back now at age seventy-three, how different our lives could have been, if we remained in Jamaica. My mother was anxious to come to America, "…Land of the free and home of the brave…," where we had so much more to learn about this world.

My mother's words, **"Hold on kids,"** held several meanings for me:

Hold on - Take in the beauty around you! Smell the roses and appreciate nature. These are God's gifts to you.

Hold on – Investigate your world. Learn all you can yet be careful. Hold hands when you cross the road and look out for others.

Hold on – To family and friends and open your heart to others you may or may not know. Diversity has such promise!

Hold on – Be prepared for challenges, educate yourself, and listen to others. There is always something new to learn.

Hold on – Be prepared to laugh, to sing, to soar into the universe.

Hold on - To music, it will bring you a lifetime of immeasurable joy.

Hold on – In health, in life, there is a deeper meaning.

Hold on – In spirit and allow the forces to hold you, embrace you, to lift you when you're down. See the wonder life has to offer.

Yes Mother, those of us left behind will hold on to your words, your faith, your hope and your love. Orlando died in 1999 from complications of an enlarged heart. The doctors in Indiana wanted him to have a heart transplant, with a fifty percent survival rate. However, Mayo Cleveland Clinic did not think that was advisable. He lived another four years. I know you know this already and you are taking good care of him. The rest of your children are holding on to life's joys and struggles, through sickness and in health. You can be assured every day of my life, I can hear your voice saying, "Hold on kids," and see your smile.

I am comforted.

My Family

Clarence & Beverley

Clarence and Mia

Norman with his young family

Orlando in his 20s

The doll for my 50th birthday

My 4H dress

Eddie on Venice Beach 2014

Younger picture of Eddie

Beverley with her favorite doll muff

www.ingramcontent.com/pod-product-compliance
Lightning Source LLC
Chambersburg PA
CBHW070005120726
47909CB00003B/805